# 240 Speaking Topics
## with
## Sample Answers

LIKE TEST PREP

ISBN: 1489544089
ISBN-13: 978-1489544087

# DEDICATION

To the LIKE Family

# Contents

# Contents

# Contents

# Contents

# Contents

# Contents

# Five Things to Think about

1. Did you answer the question?

-Start by restating the question and answer it.

2. Was your answer logical?

-A structure of an introduction, body, and conclusion is good. Present an argument and two or three supporting ideas. Also provide specific examples. Do not deviate from the topic.

3. Were you fluent?

-You do not need to use difficult words or expressions frequently to receive a high score. Instead, speak without unnecessary pauses and halts.

4. Was your speech accurate?

-Your speech needs to be accurate in terms of grammar, vocabulary use, and pronunciation. Also speak loudly and clearly.

5. Did you speak for more than 35~40 seconds?

-Try to say at least ten sentences. Organize your answer using the simple formula given on the next page.

### Independent Task: 45 Seconds

- Sentence 1: restate the question and answer the question.

- Sentence 2: Supporting Idea 1

- Sentence 3-5: Supporting Idea 1 Detail & Example

- Sentence 6: Supporting Idea 2

- Sentence 7-9: Supporting Idea 2, Detail & Example

- Sentence 10: Rephrase & Summarize.

### If You Have No Idea What to Say...

1. Write what you would want to say.

2. Ask your English Teacher to correct it for you.

3. Revise what you wrote.

4. Memo what you wrote.

5. Practice speaking only with your memo.

6. Record your speech.

# Sample Questions & Answers

Q1. What is an event you remember well, such as an anniversary or birthday? Explain why using details and examples.

The event that I remember well is my 15th birthday. On that day, all my close friends came to celebrate it. My best friends including James, David, Nina, and Rocko came, and we had a great time together having food and playing games. Another reason I remember well is that I received many expensive gifts. My friends bought me a game DVD, my brother bought me a new electronic dictionary, and my parents got me a new bicycle. My 15th birthday was great. I received the things that I always wanted and my best friends and I had a great time.

Q2. Describe the country you would most like to visit and explain why. Include details and examples to support your explanation.

I want to go to France for two reasons. First, France is known for art. France has many famous painters' works in the museums and galleries. Monet, Da Vinci, Degas and Picasso are only few of them. Secondly, France has many good food. I especially enjoy French meals and desserts such as chocolates and cakes. They are very delicious. As France has many places to visit and great food to eat, it would be the country I would most like to visit.

Q3. What is the most important holiday in your country? Why do you think it is so important? Include details and examples to support your explanation.

The New Year's Day is the most important holiday in my country. There are two reasons for this. The New Year's Day is the first traditional holiday of the year, and people gather with their family members and relatives. They visit their ancestral tombs, share food, and play traditional games such as Yutnori together. Another reason is that on this day, people make new resolutions. Some vow to quit smoking, when some decide to pass the college entrance exam. As people spend this day with close ones and think seriously about their future, the New Year's Day is the most important holiday in my country.

## Q121. Which season – winter, spring, summer, or fall – is your favorite?

_____
_____
_____
_____
_____
_____

### A. Sample Answer

My favorite season is winter because of two reasons. First, Christmas is in winter and I always love getting presents from my family. Usually, on Christmas, I get toys from my sister and chocolate from my mother. We always have a great time together on Christmas. Second, I love to play in the snow. When I was younger, I made a snow angel or a snowman every year on the first day it snowed. I still do it today. In winter, I also get to see my little brother throw a snowball at my dad. It's very funny. Since it is a great season to spend with my family, I think winter is my favorite season.

### B. Create new sentences using the expressions below.

(1) one's favorite

_____

(2) love ... ing (cf. love to + verb)

_____

(3) have a good time ~ing

_____

(4) a wonderful place to visit

_____

### C. Find an error in each sentence.

(1) At Christmas, we get together and sing Christmas carol.

(2) We had a great time to play hide and seek in the woods.

(3) On the first day it snowed last year, we made snowballs and threw them for each other.

(4) I still remember to play in the snow with my sisters when I was very young.

## Q122. If you could plan the perfect day to spend with your close friends, where would you go and why?

_____

_____

_____

_____

_____

_____

### A. Sample Answer

If I could plan the perfect day to spend with my friends, I would go to Paris. Paris is a great city, filled with a lot of opportunities. First, we could go shopping in the Galeries Lafayette. We could buy lots of expensive perfumes, sweaters, scarves, and jeans. We could spend hours getting lost in the wonderful department store. Also, we could eat some of the fanciest food in the world. I've always wanted to eat a baguette near the Eiffel Tower with my friends and if we were in Paris, I would love the opportunity to do so. We could even eat the baguette with some chocolate hazelnut spread. Because we could have a lot of fun, the perfect day with my friends would be in Paris.

### B. Create new sentences using the expressions below.

(1) be filled with (=be full of)

_____

(2) with something + pp

_____

(3) If I were a ...., I could .......

_____

(4) spend time ... ing

_____

### C. Find an error in each sentence.

(1) She is able of speaking Chinese fluently.

(2) My sister is capable to speak four languages.

(3) What is the matter at you?

(4) We have to do everything to protect an atmosphere.

## Q123. What is the most frightening experience you have ever had in your life?

_____

_____

_____

_____

_____

_____

### A. Sample Answer

The most frightening experience I've ever had was when I went to the dentist's office for the second time. I was six years old and I was so scared, I cried for hours. It was scary for two reasons. First of all, the dentist caused me a lot of pain on my first trip. On my first visit, they put lots of instruments in my mouth, which caused my mouth some distress. I hated the feeling of the latex gloves in my mouth; it just tasted gross. Also, we had to wait a long time in the office, so it made me all the more anxious, especially because the secretary wasn't nice. All in all, my second trip to the dentist wasn't that painful, but I will always remember how terrified I was of my visit.

### B. Create new sentences using the expressions below.

(1) be afraid of + N

_____

(2) be afraid to + V

_____

(3) shiver (tremble) with fear

_____

(4) be applauded by

_____

### C. Find an error in each sentence.

(1) The dentist caused me a lot of pain at my first visit to his office.
(2) The medical tools in the office made me all more nervous.
(3) I remember to visit the dental office when I was seven years old.
(4) You will end up in a trouble if you are not careful.

## Q124. Should a country's government tell its citizens how many children they can have?

_____
_____
_____
_____
_____

### A. Sample Answer

I think governments should tell their citizens how many children to have. To begin with, there are too many people on the Earth. The Earth now has over seven billion people and we simply do not have enough natural resources to feed, clothe, and raise more people. If we continue to have more and more children, a lot of people will starve to death. In addition, if a government sets up this policy, then we can live more comfortably. We will be able to live in larger homes instead of cramped apartments in the cities. For these reasons, I think that governments, like China, should do almost everything they can to limit the number of children people have.

### B. Create new sentences using the expressions below.

(1) protect A from B

_____

(2) replace A with B

_____

(3) take a long time to + V

_____

(4) manage to + V

_____

### C. Find an error in each sentence.

(1) You as well as I am to blame.
(2) Nobody has the authority to impose his moral views at other people.
(3) All humans have the right to do anything they like as much as they don't break the law.
(4) Please hurry up, and we will be late.

## Q125. Would you rather earn a lot of money working in a job that you don't like or earn less money doing something you enjoy.

_____
_____
_____
_____
_____
_____

### A. Sample Answer

I would prefer to work in a job that pays me more money though I don't like it. I have two reasons to support my idea. First, nobody really likes their job. Even though many people say they really enjoy the job, a job means that it's something you have to do out of duty. And I hate it when people tell me to do something. Second, I want to earn a lot of money because I want to own a big, beautiful mansion. If I get my mansion with a swimming pool and all, I would be the happiest person in the world. For these reasons, I would take the job that I don't like, but pays well.

### B. Create new sentences using the expressions below.

(1) be satisfied with

_____

(2) have a life worth living

_____

(3) live a fast life

_____

(4) one's view of life

_____

### C. Find an error in each sentence.

(1) He made every effort with no avail.
(2) It depends on one's view on life whether he is happy or not.
(3) He has a cheerful outlook for life.
(4) The happiest person is satisfied for both his job and income.

## Q126. Should students work while they study?

_____
_____
_____
_____
_____
_____

### A. Sample Answer

I don't think students should work while they study. If students work while they study, it will take up a bunch of time. Studying is considered an occupation, and I think that if more people treated school like a regular job with a 40-hour work week, students would learn more and be more productive. Adding work into the mix would just stress students out and make them do badly in school. Also, most jobs for students are really bad, like being a janitor or a store clerk. I don't think those jobs are appealing and most don't make that much money anyway. For these two reasons, I don't think students should work while they study.

### B. Create new sentences using the expressions below.

(1) lie in (reside in)

_____

(2) live (lead) a life

_____

(3) feel regret

_____

(4) turn out

_____

### C. Find an error in each sentence.

(1) I think students should not work while they study

(2) My father told me that he was unable studying hard because he had to work to support the family.

(3) He didn't allow me working part time at a gas station.

(4) He thinks his work deprives him from his liberty.

## Q127. Which do you think is better for the environment: to build fewer factories or to create more wildlife preservation areas?

_____
_____
_____
_____
_____
_____

### A. Sample Answer

I believe we should build fewer factories rather than create more wildlife preservation areas. We have a fundamental problem with pollution and it is because we create too many things we don't need. Creating wildlife preservation areas will not solve the problem. If we build fewer factories, we will at least slow the gradual degradation of the ozone layer and our natural world. In addition, factories produce a lot of air pollution, which reaches everywhere on Earth. Smog doesn't know land boundaries, and if we build wildlife preservation areas while building more factories, the animals will eventually die off anyway from a lack of oxygen. To conclude, I argue that we should build fewer factories.

### B. Create new sentences using the expressions below.

(1) pose a great threat to

_____

(2) take a proper step to V

_____

(3) take a strong measure against

_____

(4) to stop reckless deforestation

_____

### C. Find an error in each sentence.

(1) Creating more wildlife preservation areas are not enough to improve the environment.
(2) Atmosphere is getting more and more polluted with the toxic fumes from the cars.
(3) Advacned countires hold meetings to discuss about the polluion problems regularly.
(4) The owner of the factory heavily fined for repeatedly emitting toxic marerials.

**Q128. Do you agree or disagree with the following statement? It is healthier for children to live in the countryside than in the city.**

_____
_____
_____
_____
_____

## A. Sample Answer

Parents should not scold their children in public. First off, scolding a child in public is very harmful to children. If a child gets scolded in public, it will damage his or her psyche. It is just too embarrassing for a child to withstand and if parents are too rough with a child, they can even embarrass themselves too. Secondly, a parent should always love his or her child. There is never a reason for a parent to yell or scream at a child, even if the child misbehaves. Instead, a parent should speak calmly and take control of the situation coolly. Children naturally follow their parents anyway, so parents don't have to do much to get their children to behave.

## B. Create new sentences using the expressions below.

(1) scold one for

_____

(2) in private / in public

_____

(3) do one a favor

_____

(4) for nothing

_____

## C. Find an error in each sentence.

(1) Scolding a child in public is very harmful, even traumatic, on the child.
(2) A wise mother will wisely deal with her child in the public.
(3) My big brother deals with electronic goods at his shop downtown.
(4) Jimmy seems to waste a lot times.

## Q129. Should students consult their parents about their majors and careers?

_____
_____
_____
_____
_____
_____

### A. Sample Answer

I think students should consult their parents about their majors and careers. To start with, parents are very knowledgeable about life. They have lived a lot longer than us and have more experience. If we as students consult them, we are sure to get expert advice about what to do, and we will definitely go in the right direction. Also, parents are great resources whom are very different. Some people prefer to consult just their friends, but our friends are just way too similar to us. We should get different perspectives about our majors and careers from different people, including our parents. For these reasons, I think students should consult their parents when deciding their majors and careers.

### B. Create new sentences using the expressions below.

(1) major in

_____

(2) develop into

_____

(3) get advice from

_____

(4) be well versed in

_____

### C. Find an error in each sentence.

(1) My parents exchanged their views on my majors, only showed opposing opinions.
(2) More experienced people will surely provide us for valuable opinions
(3) My parents seriously discussed about my future major.
(4) Students are supposed to abide with the school regulations.

## Q130. In order to get healthy, should people exercise more or sleep more?

_____
_____
_____
_____
_____

### A. Sample Answer

People need to sleep more in order to get healthy. Sleeping is important for two major reasons. First, sleeping rids the body of harmful toxins in the brain. When we go to sleep, the body starts to rid itself of poisons all over. If we don't go to sleep, our bodies will never be able to remove these dangerous chemicals. Also, sleeping helps recharge the body. When we go to sleep, we help conserve energy for our busy day. Sometimes, people go to work without having slept for long, but they always feel sluggish and tired and don't feel very good. Therefore, people should sleep more to be healthy.

### B. Create new sentences using the expressions below.

(1) be in good health/ be in good shape

_____

(2) take a good sleep / get enough sleep

_____

(3) suffer lack of sleep

_____

(4) go to sleep

_____

### C. Find an error in each sentence.

(1) In order to get health, we should sleep well.

(2) The word 'insomnia' means sleeplessness, with its root from Latin.

(3) Sleeping helps the body to rid itself from toxic materials accumulated in it.

(4) Some people who go to work without sleeping well are apt to fall sluggish in the office.

## Q131. If you could give a meaningful gift to a family member, what would it be?

_____

_____

_____

_____

_____

_____

### A. Sample Answer

If I could give a meaningful gift to a family member, I would give a camera to my sister. My sister loves photography. All she wants to do is take pictures and her old camera is outdated. She needs a better camera to help improve her skills and even though the camera would be expensive, it would be worth it. Also, we could make a lot of memories. My sister could take pictures when we go on vacation to Paris, London, or Hong Kong. Or, when we have a special occasion like a wedding, she could take special pictures. Because it could help her realize her dream of becoming a photographer, I would give my sister a camera as a meaningful gift.

### B. Create new sentences using the expressions below.

(1) make up for

_____

(2) realize one's dream

_____

(3) outdated

_____

(4) say a prayer that~

_____

### C. Find an error in each sentence.

(1) A: Here is something to you.

   B: Wow! That's exactly that I wanted, thanks a lot.

(2) All you have to do is studying hard.

(3) The antic is worth of $1.000.

(4) His speech, though brief, was worthy praise.

## Q132. Explain your learning style: visual, auditory, kinesthetic, etc.

_____

_____

_____

_____

_____

### A. Sample Answer

For me, I find that I learn the most when I see something. When I see something, I can almost always remember it. That's why it really helps me when the teacher uses the board. I often don't take notes, but it's not because I'm not a good student; it's simply because I don't need to. I just have a very good written memory. For example, my teacher wrote very complex math problems on the board and even though I didn't take notes, I got a 100% on my exam. Sometimes, I'll even take notes for myself, read them, and then throw them out. I'm just a great visual learner and that's the way my brain works.

### B. Create new sentences using the expressions below.

(1) the way one does something

_____

(2) That's why ......

_____

(3) take notes

_____

(4) jot down

_____

### C. Find an error in each sentence.

(1) Different people have different idea.

(2) A: Welcome to home, honey. I 've prepared your favorite dish for dinner.

    B: That's why I thank you all the time.

(3) During the classes, Jenny takes note meticulously and never shows them to others.

(4) I like the way you smile.

**Q133. What do you think are some of the causes and what are some of the solutions to the problem of obesity in today's society?**

_____

_____

_____

_____

_____

## A. Sample Answer

There are two main causes two obesity today: the widespread availability of fast food and an increased sedentary lifestyle. Fast food is all around us. What with the hundreds of Burger Kings, McDonalds, and Taco Bells just in the area alone, people are consuming too many calories without much nutrition. It is just too cheap not to eat. Increasingly, people are not exercising enough as well. The number of jobs that don't require any physical labor is also reaching an all-time high. Jobs as secretaries are increasing while jobs as farmers are decreasing. To combat both of these problems, I think people should eat less junk food and exercise more.

## B. Create new sentences using the expressions below.

(1) hard to resist

_____

(2) reduce / lose one's weight

_____

(3) put on (gain, pick up) weight

_____

(4) be on a diet

_____

## C. Find an error in each sentence.

(1) How much do you weight?

(2) Well—balanced diets are essential for you to stay you healthy

(3) More exercise is a better keeper of health than more sleeping.

(4) Regular medical checkups are also necessary to keep one in a good health.

**Q134. Do you think that seeing violence in video games or movies cause people to behave violently?**

---
---
---
---
---
---

## A. Sample Answer

I don't think seeing violence in video games or movies causes people to become violent themselves. People who behave violently often have emotional problems. Even though these kinds of people are more likely to consume violent media, that does not mean the media itself causes violent behavior. Correlation does not mean causation, after all. And secondly, some people play violent video games like Halo or Call of Duty simply to relieve stress. With all of the stresses of modern society, some teenagers just need to get away and blow off steam. These two reasons are why I don't think people become violent after watching violent movies or playing violent video games.

## B. Create new sentences using the expressions below.

(1) cause A to V

_____

(2) be likely to V

_____

(3) need to

_____

(4) be influenced by

_____

## C. Find an error in each sentence.

(1) The boxer was strung up before the game.

(2) Some sensitive children tends to be easily influenced by violent video games.

(3) The two countries are still in a tense relation.

(4) Most of people in the town are not safe from violent gangsters.

## Q135. Should children be allowed to eat only the foods they want?

_____

_____

_____

_____

_____

_____

### A. Sample Answer

I think children should be allowed to only eat food they want to eat. First, children are known for making good food choices. Every little kid I know around me would prefer to eat fruits and vegetables over chocolate and candy. In my experience, children really like to eat spinach, cabbage, and carrots, and they naturally gravitate towards these at the supermarket. Also, kids are not picky; they just have certain foods they don't like, and parents should not force them to eat foods they don't like. Even parents have certain foods they don't like. For example, my mom doesn't like pineapple. I would never force her to eat pineapple, and she shouldn't force anyone else to eat it either.

### B. Create new sentences using the expressions below.

(1) be allowed to

_____

(2) be known for/be famous for

_____

(3) force (enforce/urge) one to V

_____

(4) be picky about

_____

### C. Find an error in each sentence.

(1) He is too fastidious. He is really hard to be pleased.
(2) We had a lot of trouble to solve the problem.
(3) The members had a lot of difficulties to draw a conclusion.
(4) The campers had a wonderful time together to dance and sing.

## Q136. Should children be given the freedom to dress anyway they want?

_____
_____
_____
_____
_____
_____

### A. Sample Answer

Children should be allowed to dress anyway they want. Children need to feel creative, and one way parents can encourage their children to experiment and do different things is to let them dress themselves. One of my little cousins mixed bright colors like orange, pink, and green for two months, and she looked fantastic. Children also need to feel secure with their fashion choices too. If parents criticize their fashion choices, they will have low self-esteem and then they might feel very sad whenever somebody makes fun of them. I think letting children dress themselves is an important part of a child's development.

### B. Create new sentences using the expressions below.

(1) be permitted to/be allowed to

_____

(2) look fantastic (beautiful, gorgeous)

_____

(3) feel secure with

_____

(4) in vogue (in fashion)

_____

### C. Find an error in each sentence.

(1) My brother often makes fun at me for my exotic fashion choice.
(2) He was jeered by his friends for his foolish behavior.
(3) We should be open-minded towards other people's tastes of fashion.
(4) An old saying went, "So many people so many minds."

## Q137. Would you save your money at a bank or at your home? Why?

_____

_____

_____

_____

_____

_____

### A. Sample Answer

I prefer to save money at home rather than in a bank. If we save our money at a bank, we won't have easy access to our money. Saving our money at a bank means that we might have to travel far away in order to withdraw money. However, by keeping our money at home, we can always access our money conveniently, which is much better than a bank far away. In addition, I have a lot of money. I don't think I can trust other people with my money, especially a bank. They might just try to steal from me. Therefore, I think it is better to save money at home rather than in a bank.

### B. Create new sentences using the expressions below.

(1) deposit money at a place /deposit money with a person

_____

(2) have easy access to

_____

(3) withdraw money from

_____

(4) prefer to V

_____

### C. Find an error in each sentence.

(1) Saving money with a bank is safer than keeping it at home.
(2) A man robbed money from the bank.
(3) In fall, the trees are stripped with their leaves.
(4) The high-ranking offical was deprived from his position.

**Q138. If you could choose your own study hour, how many hours would you study?**

_____

_____

_____

_____

_____

### A. Sample Answer

I would choose to study two hours a day in addition to school. I have two reasons why. My first reason is that I only really need to study for chemistry and math. I'm really terrible at those subjects, so if I just spend a little bit of time everyday studying those two subjects, I can improve my grade significantly. My second reason is that I'm really busy. I have a part-time job at my local coffee shop and I have numerous extracurricular activities, including a soccer team and a volunteer club. I also have to help out around the house, so I just don't have that much time to waste. For these reasons, if I could choose my own study hours, I would only study for two hours a day.

### B. Create new sentences using the expressions below.

(1) in addition to

_____

(2) choose to

_____

(3) spend time ...ing

_____

(4) have no time to waste

_____

### C. Find an error in each sentence.

(1) I take a piano lesson every other days

(2) I like to help Mom for chores around the house

(3) Most children in Korea are so busy to attend many private classes after school

(4) My brother is so busy now with doing his homework

## Q139. Do you think it's important for children to learn how to swim at an early age?

_____
_____
_____
_____
_____
_____

### A. Sample Answer

I don't think it's important for children to learn to swim when they're young. First, we don't really need to know how to swim. One of my friends, Molly, does not know how to swim and she never needed to learn. She always lived in the city, where there wasn't a lot of water or swimming pools available. Swimming just never interested her. Second, it's not hard to learn how to swim. One of my friends learned how to swim in college. She took a class and it only took her a couple of tries before she was doing all kinds of moves in the water, like the backstroke. In conclusion, I don't think it's important for children to learn to swim at a young age.

### B. Create new sentences using the expressions below.

(1) learn to V = learn how to V

_____

(2) available

_____

(3) A interests B = B is interested in A

_____

(4) important for somebody to V

_____

### C. Find an error in each sentence.

(1) While travelling through Europe, I was greatly interested for the buildings in Rome

(2) There're four swimming styles. I am especially good for backstroke

(3) I'm good at English, but rather poor in mathematic

(4) My sister is a good swimmer. I am envious in her

**Q140. Should older children learn to cook so they can help prepare the family meals sometimes?**

_____

_____

_____

_____

_____

_____

## A. Sample Answer

Older children should not learn to cook at all. To start with, there's no need to learn how to cook. Because there are so many restaurants, nobody needs to know how to cook nowadays. You can simply go to a restaurant anytime you are hungry and eat something. You can even order food over the phone or the Internet and have it delivered. Also, even older children might get hurt when cooking. Cooking can be dangerous; we can get burned from the stove or even cut ourselves with a knife. Then, we might end up in the hospital, and that would not be fun. Therefore, I don't think that older children should learn how to cook.

## B. Create new sentences using the expressions below.

(1) get hurt

_____

(2) get burned

_____

(3) end up ... ing

_____

(4) cook the books (=flasify books=cook accounts)

_____

## C. Find an error in each sentence.

(1) Have you heard the old saying, "Too many cookers spoil the broth" ?

(2) I don't like too spicy food. It's pungent taste burns my tongue.

(3) The ceremony was participating with many dignitaries.

(4) He came up on a new recipe. His food sells like hot cakes.

## Q141. Which skill do you think is more important in foreign language learning?

_____
_____
_____
_____
_____
_____

### A. Sample Answer

The most important skill in foreign language learning is reading. Reading allows us to do many things on our own, so it can help us to be independent. For example, when I am at a restaurant, I can't have the waiter read off a menu to me; that would be rude. We just have to know how to read to do these kinds of simple tasks. However, we can always ask someone to write something down like directions to the zoo or instructions on how to do something. In addition, reading is usually easier. Sometimes it's hard to speak because the sounds are difficult to make. However, we shouldn't have any trouble writing things down. Because of these two reasons, I think reading is the most important skill when learning a foreign language.

### B. Create new sentences using the expressions below.

(1) be fascinated with

_____

(2) have a good commend of

_____

(3) have trouble ...ing

_____

(4) on one's own

_____

### C. Find an error in each sentence.

(1) Reading is most important foreign language skill

(2) It is rude having a stranger read the menu for you.

(3) Leaning a foreign language is likened to travel to a strange land.

(4) Few student is absent today.

**Q142. Which is your favorite ethnic (Italian, Chinese, Korean, Mexican, French, etc.) food?**

_____

–
_____

–
_____

–
_____

–
_____

–
_____

–

**A. Sample Answer**

My favorite ethnic food is Thai food because of two reasons. To start off, my favorite dish is Thai curry. It is always really delicious and I love the many different flavors involved in making it like green onions, ginger, and coconut milk. It is creamy, yet spicy, and that's something I like. Plus, there are so many ways to make Thai curry; I never get bored of it. Also, Thai food is almost always easy to a vegetarian. I'm not a vegetarian, but I am trying not to eat meat as often as I once did. It's healthier that way, and Thai food can really help me to stay healthy. For these reasons, Thai food is my favorite ethnic food.

**B. Create new sentences using the expressions below.**

(1) one's favorite ethnic food

_____

(2) run a cooking school

_____

(3) kitchen utensils

_____

(4) how to make kimchi

_____

**C. Find an error in each sentence.**

## Q143. Laughter and joy are essential aspects for a healthy life. Why or why not?

_____
_____
_____
_____
_____
_____

### A. Sample Answer

I don't think laughter and joy are essential for a healthy life. First off, laughing can sometimes be inappropriate. For example, I went to a funeral with one of my friends. His mom had died just two months before and the funeral was for his dead sister. He started laughing uncontrollably, and that was not very good. People thought he was crazy. In addition, some people live very successful lives while having no sense of humor. Think about most college professors. They are very dedicated to their work, always eat healthy, and yet have no sense of humor. Therefore, I think that laughter and joy are not necessarily needed for life, though they do make things more interesting.

### B. Create new sentences using the expressions below.

(1) meet the requirements

_____

(2) make both ends meet

_____

(3) be badly off

_____

(4) devote oneself to

_____

### C. Find an error in each sentence.

(1) My uncle has a sense of humor; His humor makes people around him to laugh happily.
(2) John played an important role in the meeting and was elected as the president of the club
(3) The meeting is scheduled on the next Sunday.
(4) All the regular members are required for attendance

## Q144. When you feel sad, what are some things you do to help yourself feel better?

_____

_____

_____

_____

_____

_____

_____

### A. Sample Answer

When I feel sad, there are two things I do to help myself feel better. First, I always cry. Crying always helps me to get out my emotions. When I cry, I feel a huge burden being lifted and I no longer have to keep my emotions bottled up. Second, I make sure to talk to my mom. My mom always gives me the best hugs and she always makes me feel better. Sometimes, she will make me hot chocolate, and other times, she will give me the best advice in the world. Without my mom, I don't know what I would do. When I feel sad, I always cry and talk to my mom to make myself feel better.

### B. Create new sentences using the expressions below.

(1) a load on one's mind

_____

(2) be relieved of

_____

(3) shoulder a burden

_____

(4) give one a hug (a kiss)

_____

### C. Find an error in each sentence.

(1) When I feel sad, I always turn around to my mom for comfort.
(2) He lives up to his word without any fail.
(3) He has no body around him to talk freely.
(4) Crying often makes one relieved from worries.

## Q145. Do you think it's a good idea to loan money to friends?

## A. Sample Answer

I don't think it's a good idea to give loan to friends. To begin, most friends you loan money to are poor. If they were rich, they would never ask for money in the first place. Therefore, it's especially risky to loan money to friends because they might not be serious enough to pay you back. I also don't think that friends would spend the money wisely. Most teenagers nowadays spend too much money on clothes, food, and other things they don't need. They just rack up a lot of debt that their parents must pay off. For these reasons, I don't think that it' a good idea to loan money to friends.

## B. Create new sentences using the expressions below.

(1) make sentences using 'lend' and 'borrow' respectively

_____

(2) take something seriously

_____

(3) be wise with

_____

(4) repay (a loan, one's kindness)

_____

## C. Find an error in each sentence.

(1) I don't think it is wise to borrow money to an unfaithful friend.
(2) If I were rich now, I could have bought a ferrari.
(3) He lives on the 10<sup>th</sup> street.
(4) How long have you been away on the vacation?

**Q146. Is it important to have expensive but beautiful things such as fancy cars and designer label clothes?**

_____
_____
_____
_____
_____
_____
_____

## A. Sample Answer

It's not important to have expensive and beautiful things for two important reasons. First off, most expensive things are really not worth the price. I think that we have to be humble; for me, what's most important about a car is whether or not it functions correctly, not whether it looks beautiful or is expensive. Therefore, paying lots of money for a car is useless because cheaper cars exist. Also, more people will hate you if you have expensive things. Having designer label clothes makes you hated by a lot of people. I know once I wore a Prada scarf and people came up to me and called me a snob. Therefore, I don't think that we even should have these sorts of pricy items.

## B. Create new sentences using the expressions below.

(1) be worth

_____

(2) call one a bad name

_____

(3) lack efficiency in one's work

_____

(4) look good in a dress/a dress looks good on somebody

_____

## C. Find an error in each sentence.

(1) The new dress is becoming with you.
(2) Your red necktie goes on your blue shirt.
(3) Her new dress is not worthy the price. I think she was overcharged.
(4) The tailor said to me, "Just try in this suit."

## Q147. What is your favorite type of exercise?

_____

_____

_____

_____

_____

_____

### A. Sample Answer

My favorite type of exercise is playing soccer. I have two reasons to support my opinion. Firstly, I can play with many people I don't know. Since soccer is a team sport, I can play with my friends and learn good sportsmanship. Soccer is a great way for me to meet people, and it's how I met people when I first came to America. Secondly, playing soccer involves a good mixture of cardio. There is a lot of running, jumping, kicking, and other moves. These kinds of exercises help keep me slim and trim and can even help me get a six pack. For these reasons, my favorite exercise is playing soccer.

### B. Create new sentences using the expressions below.

(1) one's favorite type of exercise

_____

(2) grow familiar with

_____

(3) get used to

_____

(4) used to + V

_____

### C. Find an error in each sentence.

(1) Soccer provides a great way to me to get together with many people.
(2) He was used to work out at a gym.
(3) Jogging is the one of the best ways to keep one in good shape.
(4) Overworking is dangerous more than doing nothing.

## Q148. When you choose a friend, which quality is more important in that person: honesty or physical appearance?

_____
_____
_____
_____
_____
_____
_____

### A. Sample Answer

Physical appearance is more important when choosing a friend. If we are not friends with pretty people, we will not be popular and therefore, we might jeopardize potential new friendships. For example, I was once friends with an ugly person, and then nobody wanted to be friends with me. Being popular is just too important. Also, if we have beautiful friends, then we can get free stuff. People give out free food, drinks, and toys to other people they think are pretty. If we have only beautiful friends, then we might get some of that free stuff too. For these reasons, I prefer to choose my friends based on how they look.

### B. Create new sentences using the expressions below.

(1) be eligible for

_____

(2) be qualified to

_____

(3) be popular with

_____

(4) what's more (=in addition)

_____

### C. Find an error in each sentence.

(1) If I had studied harder, I could pass the test then.

(2) If Jack were here on our team, we could have beaten our opponents easily.

(3) The pilot was sick in the bed, but his heart was high in the air.

(4) Jessica is an object of envy among her friends. Everybody is envious for her.

## Q149. If there was a fire or some other type of disaster in your house, what would you take with you? Why?

_____

_____

_____

_____

_____

_____

### A. Sample Answer

If there were a disaster in my house, I would absolutely take my phone with me. If I take my phone with me, then I won't have to pay a lot of money to replace it when I make it out of my burning house. A phone costs a lot of money to replace and if I don't take it with me, then I might have to settle for a phone of lesser quality. Also, if I take my phone, it can help me get into contact with my family members. My family members are the most important people in my life and I want to make sure that they're all right. If they take their phones with them, then we will know they're OK and help comfort one another. For these reasons, I would take my phone with me if there were a disaster.

### B. Create new sentences using the expressions below.

(1) get in touch with

_____

(2) keep in contact with

_____

(3) cost one a lot of money

_____

(4) make sure that + clause

_____

### C. Find an error in each sentence.

(1) Don't forget to take your mom tomorrow, Mary. I have something to talk about with her.
(2) Please bring this book to the library.
(3) The runner who came in the last received a hearty cheer from the spectators.
(4) The runner from Uganda came in the second.

## Q150. Who is your best friend? Why is he/she important to you?

_____

_____

_____

_____

_____

_____

### A. Sample Answer

My best friend is a girl I met in Korea named Christina. She is important to me for two reasons. Firstly, she and I love to do things together. We like to travel, eat meals, and work out together. We always do fun things with one another, practically every day. We just share so many of the same interests, including television shows. Every Sunday night, we even get together to make popcorn and watch Mad Men. We always have a fun time. In addition, Christina is someone I can really depend on. Whenever I get anxious about being in Korea or feel a little sad, Christina is always there to help cheer me up. Without her, I just would not know what to do. Because Christina is so dependable and so much fun, she is my best friend in Korea.

### B. Create new sentences using the expressions below.

(1) a place named....

_____

(2) a movie titled.....

_____

(3) have many things in common

_____

(4) depend on

_____

### C. Find an error in each sentence.

(1) I'm going to the movie with my friends in the afternoon.

(2) Then we will enjoy wonderful dinner at an Italian restaurant.

(3) My parents are going out to a friend's place for supper. They'll stay there late at night.

(4) More people than ever are interested in study of Chinese.

## Q151. If you could be famous for something, what would you want to be famous for?

_____

_____

_____

_____

_____

_____

### A. Sample Answer

If I could be famous for anything, I would want to be famous for the discovery of life on other planets. The first reason for this is that it would allow me to gain recognition from the scientific community. if I discovered life on other planets, I could act as a fatherly figure to that life. I would have a special bond with the extraterrestrials and could ensure that they stay on my side. Being the father of a whole new species of people would make me extremely powerful. Maybe I could even colonize their planet and establish myself as the ruler. Then, I would not only be famous for discovering new life, but establishing the first government on a planet other than Earth as well. So, to conclude, I would love to be famous for discovering life on another planet.

### B. Create new sentences using the expressions below.

(1) If I could.... , I would make.....

_____

(2) allow one to V

_____

(3) put up with (=to bear, to stand)

_____

(4) look upon A as B

_____

### C. Find an error in each sentence.

(1) I would not only be famous for creating a new space rocket, also but establish myself as a great space traveler.

(2) She established herself for a great pianist in her early 20's.

(3) Rome is famous for the ancient capital of the Roman Empire.

(4) San Francisco is well known as the Golden Gate Bridge.

## Q152. Do you think teenagers should be allowed to drive?

_____

_____

_____

_____

### A. Sample Answer

I do think that teenagers should be allowed to drive for two very important reasons. First off, teenagers need to be able to drive to do important errands for their family. When I was a teenager, I always did things for my mom and dad. I drove my little siblings around after school to things like doctors' appointments and play dates. I also frequently drove to the grocery store because my mom would forget something important like butter or cheese for dinner. In general, teenagers should be able to drive so they can do things for other people. Additionally, teenagers need to be able to drive in order to get practice. Some of my friends didn't drive when they were teens. They are having a very difficult time now learning because they didn't learn when they were younger. Had their parents encouraged them to drive when they were, say, 16 or 17, they would have saved a lot of time and energy as adults. Accordingly, I think that teenagers should be allowed to drive.

### B. Create new sentences using the expressions below.

(1) be able to V….

_____

(2) be capable of ….ing

_____

(3) so that …. can

_____

(4) Had it not been for, … would have pp. ….

_____

### C. Find an error in each sentence.

(1) Passed the test, my sister was issued a driver's license.

(2) Minors should not be allowed driving a car.

(3) Have it not been for you, I would have drowned.

(4) He had a difficult time to answer the questions.

## Q153. If you could meet one world leader, who would it be?

_____
_____
_____
_____
_____
_____

### A. Sample Answer

If I could meet one world leader, it would have to be Barack Obama. The first reason is that Barack Obama is basically the most powerful man in the world. Barack Obama is the President of the United States, which is one of the largest and most economically powerful nations on the globe. Meeting President Obama would open many doors for me, and allow me to get in contact with many other people, like important journalists and other celebrities. In addition, President Obama is one of the most inspiring people in American politics. He was raised by his grandparents in a middle class home and despite many obstacles, he became editor of the Harvard Law Review, which is one of the most prestigious law journals in the United States. He also became a great constitutional law professor and even taught at the University of Chicago. In summary, I want to meet President Obama because he is one of the most powerful and inspiring leaders in the world living today.

### B. Create new sentences using the expressions below.

(1) get in touch with

_____

(2) the most prestigious/the most celebrated

_____

(3) in return for

_____

(4) be born and grow up in

_____

### C. Find an error in each sentence.

(1) He was born in a small village in Africa and grown up in Indonesia.
(2) He was elected as the Predient of the country in his early forties.
(3) Who is the most influential figure in White House?
(4) He is well known as his good judgement.

**Q154. Which do you think is better, going to college right after high school or after taking a few years off?**

_____

_____

_____

_____

**A. Sample Answer**

I think it is better to go to college after taking a few years off for two reasons. First off, high school is very stressful. There are a lot of quizzes, tests, and homework that children have to do. The high school exit exams in particular are very nerve-wracking; you have to study for hours and hours on end, memorizing a lot of material. Kids just need a little break from studying in order to stay mentally stable. In addition, taking a few years off allows students to explore many different opportunities. One of my best friends did an internship in New York during his gap year. He was able to get a lot of experience and a lot of perspective on the world before going to college. One of my other friends did his military service before going to college; he was very happy about this because he made so many friends. Because students need a break to explore many of life's possibilities, I think students should take a few years off before starting college.

**B. Create new sentences using the expressions below.**

(1) take (days, months or years) off

_____

(2) are under (a) heavy burden(s) of

_____

(3) take a break from

_____

(4) do one's military service

_____

**C. Find an error in each sentence.**

(1) Students are forcing to do a lot of things.

(2) The internship at a company hepled me a lot finding my aptitude to my future job.

(3) Finished his military service, he returned to college.

(4) Everybody need a period of break from his routine work to recharge himself.

## Q155. Which do you think is better - to live on campus or to rent an apartment off campus?

_____
_____
_____
_____
_____

### A. Sample Answer

For me, I would always choose to rent an apartment off campus rather than live on campus. The first reason why is very simple: it is cheaper. Living on campus is more expensive because you are usually located in a closer area to campus. This is expensive, especially because the college adds extra expenses you don't need like cable television. It's simply too much to afford, and by living on campus, we can save more money to have fun. Secondly, renting an apartment off campus means fewer rules. When we live on campus, we have to obey a curfew. If we break curfew and stay out past 11 o'clock, we will get reprimanded by the headmaster. However, by renting an apartment off campus, we can stay out as much as we want and meet lots of interesting characters on the street well past midnight. Because it is cheaper and less restrictive, I prefer to live in an apartment off campus.

### B. Create new sentences using the expressions below.

(1) rent a room

_____

(2) be economical / expensive

_____

(3) obey a rule

_____

(4) plead guilty

_____

### C. Find an error in each sentence.

(1) Nowadays things are changing for better.
(2) Children are trying to live up for their parents' expectations.
(3) Thanks for his brother's help, John could get a high mark on his mathematics test.
(4) Living off campus means that a student lives in a renting house or an apartment.

**Q156. Some people prefer going to a movie theater instead of watching a movie at home. Which do you prefer? Why?**

_____
_____
_____
_____
_____
_____

## A. Sample Answer

I definitely prefer to watch a movie in a movie theater for two very important reasons. Firstly, there are too many distractions at home. When I'm at home, there is always somebody doing something. My mom might be cooking or my little sister might listen to her music without headphones. Even though there are other people making some noises in the movie theater, it in no way matches the noise made in my home on a daily basis. The second reason is that all of the current movies are available in the movie theater. Although going to the movie theater is more expensive, if we watch a movie at home, then we can only watch movies that came out after a year or so. Instead, the best place to go to watch the newest features is the cinema. For these two reasons, I prefer to watch a movie in theaters.

## B. Create new sentences using the expressions below.

(1) pluck up one's courage

_____

(2) as pleased as punch (= very pleased)

_____

(3) pledge alligence (to)

_____

(4) be ideal for

_____

## C. Find an error in each sentence.

(1) "I hope I'm not disturbing you, Miss Brown.", said Mr. Johnson knocking the door.
(2) Don't hesitate to contact with me.
(3) Never before I have played tennis.
(4) Rarely he plays the piano.

## Q157. What is your favorite way to spend your free time?

_____

_____

_____

_____

_____

### A. Sample Answer

My absolute favorite way to spend my free time is to read books. To start off, by reading books, we can relax a lot. Unlike exercising or taking a walk, reading books takes really no energy. It's almost like sleeping, except we are awake. When we read, there are no noises or anything else to distract us; it is just peace and quiet with none of the stresses of modern day life. It kind of reminds me of what it was like in the olden days. Also, reading books allows me to go on a journey. I can imagine a lot of different places and people when I start reading a new book. For example, I started reading The Hobbit a couple of days ago. Whenever I read The Hobbit, I love imagining myself as a passive spectator, fascinated just by the different worlds like The Elven Kingdom or The Shire. I love being able to transport myself to a different world through books. To conclude, because books are relaxing and transport me to another world, my favorite way to spend my free time is reading books.

### B. Create new sentences using the expressions below.

(1) in favor of

_____

(2) curry favor with

_____

(3) be cautious of/be wary of

_____

(4) transfer to

_____

### C. Find an error in each sentence.

(1) Someone rang the doorbell while I had a shower.

(2) Love stories are my preference taste.

(3) What story impressed you best?

(4) The Chapter 10 of the book is the best part, I think.

**Q158. Some people prefer learning from books, while others prefer learning from experiences. Which one do you prefer?**

_____

_____

_____

_____

_____

### A. Sample Answer

Without a doubt, I prefer learning from books. First off, with books I can always go back and revisit things if I forget them. For example, when I was learning about chemistry, I would always forget things if they weren't written down. I forgot formulas or equations often. If I had just learned chemistry through experience, it would have been much harder for me. However, because I had a chemistry textbook, I was able to succeed and even got an A in my second semester chemistry class. Also, reading is a great way to build up vocabulary. Even though we learn a lot of things from experience, I need to learn vocabulary in order to prepare for the high school exit examinations. Regrettably, an open mind would not help me to pass my test. Because it is more useful and helps me to learn better, I prefer learning from books.

### B. Create new sentences using the expressions below.

(1) force (urge) one to do something

_____

(2) root for

_____

(3) get ready for

_____

(4) come up with

_____

### C. Find an error in each sentence.

(1) Reading is a great way to build up a vocabulary.

(2) Look it up the dictionary when you come to a new word.

(3) Mr. Peter is very imaginative. He often comes with a novel idea.

(4) What you say doesn't make much sense to me.

## Q159. Who do you admire the most?

---
---
---
---
---

### A. Sample Answer

The person I admire the most is Yu-na Kim for two very good reasons. The first reason is that Yu-na Kim is a famous celebrity. She is one of the world's best figure skaters in the world and I admire her for her talent and grace on the ice. Because she is so talented, she was able to get the attention of many people outside of South Korea. She is probably the most famous living South Korean woman out there and I love the way that she is famous for something important, rather than for simply being rich or partying. In addition, Yu-na Kim works very hard at her job. I know that she has a very rigorous training schedule and probably trains for over eight hours a day. That includes lifting weights and practicing her routines. She also has a very strict diet; in all likelihood, she probably doesn't eat any fast food and only eats healthy food like fruits and vegetables. Because she is diligent and famous, I admire Yu-na Kim the most.

### B. Create new sentences using the expressions below.

(1) hold one in respect

_____

(2) think highly of / speak highly of

_____

(3) be participated by

_____

(4)  the way that ....

_____

### C. Find an error in each sentence.

(1) I like the way she peforms on stage.
(2) We should try eating healthy food.
(3) There are ten players in our team.
(4) Those in the committee were all for the proposed bill.

## Q160. Describe an important social or political event in your country. Why do you think it is important?

_____

_____

_____

_____

### A. Sample Answer

I think one of the most important social and political events in my country was the Civil Rights Movement in the 1950's. First off, it was a signal that the discrimination in the past would no longer be tolerated. America had a long tradition of excluding many people. African-Americans, for example, were discriminated against in regards to housing, employment, and educational opportunities. When so many people came together to protest against inequality, it sent a powerful message that America would finally move towards treating everyone with respect. Additionally, the Civil Rights Movement produced one very important figure, Dr. Martin Luther King Jr. He is regarded as one of the best people of the 1950's. Even though he was controversial at the time, Dr. King is one of the most inspirational people of all time. He told people to continue to fight against injustice and his words still ring true today. Because they helped improves the lives of all Americans, I think that the Civil Rights Movement in the 1950's is one of the most important political events in American history.

### B. Create new sentences using the expressions below.

(1) one of the most famous

_____

(2) discriminate against

_____

(3) result from

_____

(4) result in

_____

### C. Find an error in each sentence.

(1) He told people fighting against the injustice.

(2) His words still ring truly in our ears.

(3) The movement in 1950's is one of the most important political incidents in the counrty.

(4) Nobody knows who is he.

## Q161. What are the advantages and disadvantages of moving to a new home?

_____
_____
_____
_____
_____

### A. Sample Answer

Moving to a new town can be both exciting and scary at the same time. One of the main advantages of moving is the excitement of reorganizing your new house. To me, it is very fun to think of where to put everything in my new home, such as my bed, toys, and posters. Also, moving to a new home can bring you closer to some family members that you don't get to see often, like the grandparents who spoil you with cookies and candies every time you visit! On the other hand, moving can be a depressing experience, especially for children who have to leave behind their friends. Another disadvantage is that you might not like the new area you move too. One example is that the weather can be a type that you particularly don't like. For example, I had to move from the beautiful hot weather of Texas, to the cold and gloomy weather of Pennsylvania. Moving can be a good thing, but it can also be a bad thing. It all depends on how you look at it and how you want to handle the changes.

### B. Create new sentences using the expressions below.

(1) both advantages and disadvantages

_____

(2) It's very fun to

_____

(3) spoil one

_____

(4) be rich in / abound in (with)

_____

### C. Find an error in each sentence.

(1) Our family moved from California to Florida ten years before.

(2) Our family had moved from Florida to California two years ago.

(3) I didn't see you for a long time, Dr. Kim.

(4) Who is do you think the best player?

## Q162. You found $20 under your desk at school. What would you do, tell the teacher or keep it?

_____

_____

_____

_____

### A. Sample Answer

If I found $20 under my desk at school, I would tell the teacher, without hesitation. My mother raised me to be a truthful person, and I would have a guilty conscience if I stole the money and didn't say anything to my teacher. First, my mother raised me to be a truthful person. Therefore, if I took the money, I would be going against the way my mother reared me. Disappointing my mother would be very difficult to do, because she worked so hard to teach us the difference between right and wrong. Stealing somebody else's money, even if we are unsure of whose money it is, is wrong. Also, my conscience would eat away at me for the rest or the school year, and years to come. By telling the truth to the teacher, she will be able to find the proper owner of the money, or judiciously distribute the money for a good cause. If I don't fess up and be honest, I would feel guilty and it would be unbearable to look at people in the eyes. Since stealing is wrong, my mother taught me better, and I would have a guilty conscience, I would without a doubt tell my teacher about a $20 bill that was under my desk and was not mine.

### B. Create new sentences using the expressions below.

(1) without hesitation

_____

(2) in time / on time

_____

(3) without a doubt

_____

(4) rid oneself of

_____

### C. Find an error in each sentence.

(1) My lad, you should tell a truth all the time.

(2) The boy was punished for telling the lie.

(3) An old saying went, 'Honesty is the best policy.'

(4) Honesty will return in the long run.

## Q163. What is your preferred place to visit on weekends?

_____
_____
_____
_____
_____

### A. Sample Answer

My preferred place to visit on the weekends is a very popular hotspot here in Korea; it's the city of Busan. Busan offers many new and exciting things to see and also my boyfriend is in Busan. To begin with, Busan offers many new and exciting things to see. Just last weekend, there was a great cultural festival that many foreigners and Koreans partook in. It was the Hali Hai festival. Busan often has cultural events that I can enjoy in, all while being in a new city that I don't currently live in. Next, my boyfriend lives in Busan, so it makes it a natural choice of where I want to spend my weekends. He currently attends a university there, but will be graduating soon. So, when I go to the city by the sea, I am able to see the man who stole my heart and learn a lot more about the Korean college life. I really enjoy strolling along through his university campus and seeing the beautiful mountain landscapes the most. Because Busan offers great cultural experiences and my significant other currently lives there, I prefer to spend most of my weekends in the wonderful city of Busan.

### B. Create new sentences using the expressions below.

(1) prefer A to B

_____

(2) take place

_____

(3) partake in/take part in

_____

(4) carry ~ to an extreme

_____

### C. Find an error in each sentence.

(1) A: I don't like opera. B: I don't, too.
(2) You had better to hurry up.
(3) What's happen?
(4) I had a trouble moving this heavy bag.

**Q164. Explain in detail your happiest childhood memory and provide reasons as to why it is your happiest.**

_____

_____

_____

_____

_____

_____

## A. Sample Answer

My happiest childhood memory was the time I spent with my grandmother during the summer. We did many things together, and she was a role model as a mother that I desperately wanted needed. To start, my grandmother and I grew very close over our summers together. Every day, she and I would go to our little garden and tend to it. We grew mint, blackberries, and other various types of vegetables. Then, we would use the produce from our hard work in teas and deserts! I got my green thumb during those great moments with my Grammy. Sharing my summer with my grandmother was my happiest childhood memory because she gave me the guidance I needed and we got to do some very memorable experiences together.

## B. Create new sentences using the expressions below.

(1) attend to (=take care of)

_____

(2) a role model as

_____

(3) an example of (patriotism, success, etc.)

_____

(4) hold a discussion about

_____

## C. Find an error in each sentence.

(1) Most of students in the class were against the new school regulations.

(2) I know neither you nor he like the story.

(3) My dog gave a birth to five puppies last week.

(4) I have headache.

## Q165. What is your most valued possession non-reflective of monetary value, but of sentimental value?

_____

_____

_____

_____

### A. Sample Answer

The most valued possession of mine that is non-reflective of monetary value, but rather of sentimental value is my mother's wedding dress. It reminds me of the love that my parents once had, and it also is something that I hope to use at my own wedding. To begin with, my mother and father have been divorced for more than 20 years, and it is often times sad to think about how much they despise each other. However, when I look at the wedding dress my mother wore that day in February 1980, I am reminded about how they were once in love. They got married too young and had three children at very early ages, so it tore their love apart from each other. Furthermore, I hope that I can alter the dress to be used at my own wedding in the future. Some might think this is a bad omen to use a dress from a failed marriage, but I respond back that if it weren't for that failed marriage, I wouldn't be alive. So, even though the wedding dress from my father and mother's wedding has bad vibes surrounding it, it is my most valued sentimental item I possess.

### B. Create new sentences using the expressions below.

(1) fit right in with (=harmonize with)

_____

(2) be reflective of

_____

(3) be married to

_____

(4) be expelled from

_____

### C. Find an error in each sentence.

(1) I am always careful in pronouncing my English correctly.
(2) I had a lunch at 8 a.m.
(3) I will have your car go again in one hour.
(4) Can you have my car repairing by tomorrow?

## Q166. Talk about a person who has inspired you. Explain why the person is an inspiration.

_____

_____

_____

_____

_____

### A. Sample Answer

A person who has inspired me is my younger sister for two main reasons. Firstly, she has struggled for almost 10 years with an incurable disease that most people don't develop until they are in their latter half of their lives. She is only 28 years old but has not been able to walk on her own without the aid of crutches for just about a decade now. Imagine being a young mom of three and not being able to hold your own children, walk about with them, and play with them, like other young mothers can do. Secondly, she never was afforded the opportunity to attend college, but now, she has taken advantage of the opportunity that was presented to her. As I said previously, she has three children, so attending university classes is a massive challenge to her. However, she leans on her husband, friends, and family for support. She always holds her head up high and doesn't listen to the others who try to discourage her from doing anything she puts her mind to. Because of her strong will, stubbornness, and persistence, I am inspired by my younger sister every day.

### B. Create new sentences using the expressions below.

(1) inspire one

_____

(2) be cured of

_____

(3) with the help of

_____

(4) discourage one from .... ing

_____

### C. Find an error in each sentence.

(1) The father tried to help his son on mathematics.

(2) He persuaded the girl to marry with him and move to Canada.

(3) He encouraged his son continuing his Ph.D. course.

(4) Many unexpected events discouraged him to persue the task.

## Q167. What is your favorite location or establishment to eat at?

_____

_____

_____

_____

### A. Sample Answer

I have had some great experiences at numerous eating establishments, but if I had to choose one as my favorite, I would have to choose Pan Asia. Pan Asia is nestled in the downtown area of Daegu on what has become known as "Way-Gook Way." This restaurant's most notable dishes are the pad thai and the crab curry. Pan Asia gives Koreans and other foreigners the ability to taste authentic Thai, Singapore, and Indian food cuisines all by a very young and talented chef. He studied cooking techniques and traveled to each of the countries of the food he prepares. The food is top notch, the atmosphere is warm and inviting, and the staff is extremely professional. The thing I enjoy the most is that every time I go there, even if it's been a month or two since my last visit, the staff remembers me! Then, they offer me a complimentary beverage or appetizer because I am a frequent customer! On another note, the head chef and owner is also one of my closest friends here in Daegu, South Korea. So I get the best of both worlds when I visit my favorite restaurant, Pan Asia. I get to see my friend and I also get to enjoy the excellently prepared food with great service.

### B. Create new sentences using the expressions below.

(1) should know better than to V

_____

(2) make a choice

_____

(3) be customary to

_____

(4) go out of style

_____

### C. Find an error in each sentence.

(1) Here John comes.
(2) There again you go.
(3) Here my bus comes.
(4) Traffic laws differ from a country to a country.

## Q168. Where in your town is a good place to have fun?

_____

– _____

_____

– _____

_____

– _____

_____

– _____

_____

– _____

_____

– _____

### A. Sample Answer

I am delighted to go to Suseong Lake to have fun. First my friend and I rent, for free, a bicycle. Then we journey along the river with a packed picnic basket of sweets and treats to the Sandy Lake. While there, we bike around the lake and select our perfect spot to sit and have our snacks. It is exhausting work, so we take our time and rest when we need to. Then, we take a walk over to the nearby amusement park where we can play carnival like games. Afterwards, we continue on down to the miniature golf course, albeit it's not the best condition, where we enjoy a short round of golf. At this point, my friend and I are completely drained, so we venture on over to our chained bikes and head back home along the river again. Sandy Lake is a whole day's adventure, where you can also eat at many different restaurants or cafes too.

### B. Create new sentences using the expressions below.

(1) hear somebody .... ing

_____

(2) have a round trip

_____

(3) visit tourist attractions

_____

(4) to preserve dignity

_____

### C. Find an error in each sentence.

## Q169. Talk about an embarrassing experience in your life and describe why it was embarrassing.

_____

_____

_____

### A. Sample Answer

The most embarrassing experience in my life was the time that I walked out of the bathroom and my skirt was stuck in my tights. It all happened on a spring day when the weather was cool, so I still needed to wear tights under my skirts. I went to a sushi restaurant with my friend and had to use the bathroom while I was there. When I left the bathroom, I noticed that people were smiling strangely at me. I didn't know why until I got to the table and my friend was laughing so hard that tears were rolling down their cheeks. I asked what was so funny; she turned me around, and pulled the bottom edge of my skirt from the elastic band of my tights. I was mortified at first, but then I just laughed about it later. I was so thankful that my friend fixed my little bathroom blunder, and also, that I was wearing tights, so nobody could see my underwear. That would have been so much worse. To this day, I am always extra cautious when leaving a bathroom if I am wearing a skirt. I check multiple times to ensure my skirt is down in all locations.

### B. Create new sentences using the expressions below.

(1) be at a loss

_____

(2) keep one's head cool (remain calm)

_____

(3) tears roll down one's cheeks

_____

(4) be thankful to A for B

_____

### C. Find an error in each sentence.

(1) How does he look like?
(2) How was the weather like?
(3) He was critical for my poem.
(4) I'm sorry. I am to be blamed.

## Q170. What is your favorite subject in school?

_____
_____
_____
_____
_____
_____

### A. Sample Answer

My favorite subject in school would have to be art. Art is one of my favorite hobbies, and also I get to create things I can take home. As I mentioned first, art is my favorite hobby, so while I'm at school, I get to do my favorite pastime activity. It is not a boring subject, like Math and Grammar, so it keeps me interested too. I love the fact that I can do something fun and interesting while I'm at school. Also, while I am in art class, I am able to create my own masterpieces. I then get to take these pieces of artwork home to share with my family. I really enjoy working with clay and water colors the most, so the days that we do those mediums are my favorite days. Because it is interesting and rewarding to me, I really am favorable to my art class while I am at school.

### B. Create new sentences using the expressions below.

(1) one's favorite subject (food, color, place, etc.)

_____

(2) be weary of

_____

(3) share A with B

_____

(4) be lost in

_____

### C. Find an error in each sentence.

(1) Is the bank opened today?

(2) It is close on Mondays.

(3) I prefer staying at home to have some activities on Sundays.

(4) I prefer to stay home rather than to go out for a walk.

## Q171. Discuss an interesting tourist attraction that you have visited.

_____
_____
_____
_____
_____
_____

### A. Sample Answer

Of the many tourist attractions that I have visited around the world, the most interesting one I have visited is Epcot in Orlando, Florida. The purpose of this theme park is to dedicate the celebration of human achievement, specifically technological innovations and international culture. You can travel through the Future World and see all the wonderful inventions that this earth has seen. Also, you can journey through the World Showcase which has eleven different countries represented. The best part is that you can eat and shop at each of these countries just like you were really there. EPCOT has mini versions of some of the most popular tourist sites from each of the eleven countries. Since I was able to learn about many different countries and innovations, I find that EPCOT is the most interesting tourist attraction that I have ever visited.

### B. Create new sentences using the expressions below.

(1) tourist attractions

_____

(2) take account of

_____

(3) take credit for

_____

(4) teem with

_____

### C. Find an error in each sentence

(1) The time-honorable city of Athens has so many historic relics.
(2) Gyeongju, the ancient capital of the Silla Kingdom, is called as a museum without walls.
(3) Taking a great pride of its long history, the city holds an annual cultural expo.
(4) The excavated relics are on the display in the museum.

## Q172. Discuss a time in your life when you felt successful due to a goal or obstacle being overcome.

_____

_____

_____

_____

_____

### A. Sample Answer

I am fortunate to have overcome many obstacles, and to have also achieved many of my goals. However, if I have to choose one to discuss where I felt successful because of it, I'd have to say that it was the being inducted into Phi Kappa Phi. Throughout my early years of school, I moved a lot from different cities and countries, so I had always been put into the 'lower level' classes. This eventually wore away my confidence in my own intelligence. However, when I went off to attend my university, I was afforded the opportunity to prove myself academically on an equal and fair playing field. I work extremely hard to achieve my goal and it all paid off in the end, because I was asked to be inducted into the fraternity. You have to be the top 10% of your senior class, or the top 7.5% of your junior class. This news sent my mind soaring and my heart skipped a bit. I had finally proven to myself that I was intelligent and that all my moving had not held me back but rather challenged me to work even harder.

### B. Create new sentences using the expressions below.

(1) be fortunate to

_____

(2) tide over

_____

(3) achieve a goal

_____

(4) save one's honor/maintain one's dignity

_____

### C. Find an error in each sentence.

(1) I take pride of my alma mater, New York University.

(2) I have to find somebody to take care for my younger sister.

(3) My grandfather decided to cut down drinking coffee.

(4) My house was located near to the museum.

## Q173. When hiring a new employee, should the employer hire a person based on their knowledge or on their experience?

_____

_____

_____

_____

_____

### A. Sample Answer

When one is hiring a new employee, they should hire somebody based on their experience rather than their knowledge. In life, knowledge is important, but having experience in something is more beneficial to a company. First, if you are a skilled technician in something, then having the experience in that field is much more useful to the company than you just having book smarts about it. Secondly, it will cost the company less money to train you as well if you already have the hands on experienced required to perform a certain job skill. If the company had to hire somebody new right from a knowledge-based institution, it would cost the company a great deal of money, because they would make many costly mistakes as they are learning. By hiring an experienced person, costs due to mistakes are decreased and the person has already proven that they have the knowledge to perform the job correctly.

### B. Create new sentences using the expressions below.

(1) be based on

_____

(2) be beneficial to

_____

(3) no matter what.... (when, who..)

_____

(4) stir feelings of (pride, shame, etc.)

_____

### C. Find an error in each sentence.

(1) He has enough knowledge performing the job.
(2) It cost him with $300,000 to build the house.
(3) How much did it cost you in building the boat?
(4) He succeed to pass the exam.

## Q174. There is such a thing as being too independent. Do you agree or disagree?

_____

_____

_____

_____

_____

_____

_____

### A. Sample Answer

There is such a thing as being too independent. To begin, independence is a great thing to have because it shows that you can do things on your own. However, being too independent can lead one to become overworked. If you are always doing the things on your own, you will feel overwhelmed by the amount of work you have taken on. For instance, when you are in a new country, you'll have to translate everything on your own, which is very time-consuming and frustrating. You will become burnt out by trying to do everything independently. This brings me to my second reason that it can lead one to have an inability to ask for help. If you become too independent, you might feel ashamed or too confident to ask for help when needed. Since one can become overwhelmed and lose the ability to ask for help, I believe there is such a thing as being too independent.

### B. Create new sentences using the expressions below.

(1) turn to one for

_____

(2) on one's own

_____

(3) make sense / stand to reason

_____

(4) be inferior to / be superior to

_____

### C. Find an error in each sentence.

(1) I finally turned to him to help me.

(2) Being independent is prerequisite to be successful for one's field.

(3) Don't hesitate in asking for professional advice from the experts.

(4) Secured the sources of professional knowledge, I set out for my own business.

## Q175. Should the mistakes a person makes in the past affect a person's future? Why or why not?

_____
_____
_____
_____
_____

### A. Sample Answer

I believe that the mistakes a person makes should affect that person's future. First, mistakes are made to be learned from. If one made a mistake, it means that they did something that they should not have been doing. Therefore, we should take the lesson learned so that we don't repeat that same mistake. As the saying goes, history repeats itself. So, why should we keep making the same mistakes when we can learn from them and not repeat them again? Furthermore, we need to learn from the mistakes made, then forget the negatives and remember the positives. We don't need to remember forever the feelings we had of failure when we made a certain mistake. Instead, we should remember the positive outcomes that we received from the aftermath of that mistake. When one learns from a mistake and continues on in a positive light, then that mistake has affected a person's future in a positive way. There is no way around our mistakes affecting our future because that is the nature of a mistake.

### B. Create new sentences using the expressions below.

(1) make a mistake/commit an error

_____

(2) have an influence on

_____

(3) cannot help ~ing

_____

(4) be derived from

_____

### C. Find an error in each sentence.

(1) He is wiser than handsome.
(2) I ran on Mary at Manhattan Satation this morning.
(3) The poor man was run over by a truck driving by a reckless man.
(4) Who was on the wheel when the car hit the guard rail?

## Q176. Describe a tactic that helps you to study better.

_____
_____
_____
_____
_____

### A. Sample Answer

I have tried many different tactics to study better, from going to a library, to sitting at a park. However, the best strategy that I have adopted for studying better is by listening to music and quizzing a friend who is learning the same thing. The first tactic is that listening to music helps to keep all the other noise distractions away from me. By playing music, such as classical or techno, I am able to drown out the noise pollution around me. There is nothing more distracting from my studying than a constant sound of people eating, chewing gum, or talking. So, when music is played in my headphones, I am able to focus more inventively on my lessons that need to be learned. The second tactic is to quiz a friend who is studying the same material. There is a saying that when you teach someone, you learn more. I hold this to be true. This is because when you are explaining something to somebody else, you are reviewing the material for better understanding, and also reinforcing it in your memory. So, the next time that you have a big test coming up, try listening to rhythmic music and quizzing a fellow friend.

### B. Create new sentences using the expressions below.

(1) be regarded as

_____

(2) when it comes to

_____

(3) be burned to the ground

_____

(4) delight in

_____

### C. Find an error in each sentence.

(1) You remind me of a boy whom I grew up together.
(2) Who is responsible of the construction of the building?
(3) The clerk is pretty rude for the shoppers.
(4) Neither of the two are my friend.

## Q177. Is 18 an appropriate age to make a decision about the future of a country, state, or city? Why or why not?

_____

_____

_____

_____

### A. Sample Answer

I know this might come as a shock, but I do not believe that 18 is an appropriate age to make a decision about the future of a country, state, or city. To start with, most 18-year olds are not even out of high school yet. Therefore, they don't really have the mentality to focus on anything but themselves and their immediate world. As a high school student, they are more concerned about their school life, and their social lives, rather than the affairs of their country, state, or city. Also, they will usually follow what their parents' beliefs are because they live under the same roof. However, after their first year of college, I feel that they will be better prepared to make these difficult decisions that affect our nation, states, and cities. When they have gone to college or university, they have met other people from outside their little worlds. This causes them to have more of an open mind to others. Therefore, they are more understanding of the larger world around them. Since 18 year olds do not have the grasp on the larger world, I believe that 18 is too young of an age to make the decisions that affect more than just their high school.

### B. Create new sentences using the expressions below.

(1) make a decision

_____

(2) be concerned about

_____

(3) be prepared to

_____

(4) have the grasp of

_____

### C. Find an error in each sentence.

(1) They are so young to make any serious decisions.

(2) Nobody know what will happen tomorrow.

(3) High schoolers are not yet prepared in facing the difficulties outside their little worlds.

(4) She will come to age next year.

**Q178. Libraries, bookstores, coffee shops, parks, and other locations are where people study. Where is your favorite place to study and why?**

_____
_____
_____
_____

## A. Sample Answer

Of all the places mentioned in the statement, my bedroom is the place that I am most fond of studying at. It offers two main benefits over the other numerous options. The first of them is that it is a quiet place to study. When I have no distractions in my bedroom because it is where I get dressed and sleep only. Having no distractions, such as noisy conversations, TV, or other unexpected sounds helps me to focus on my materials that are in front of me. The second reason why my bedroom is my favorite place to study is that it has easy access to food and a bathroom. If I am studying at a library, I'd have to leave it to go get food, since no food or drinks are usually allowed in libraries. Furthermore, I'd have to take my belongings with me to use a restroom. In my room, I can freely get up, leave my belongings where they are, and even bring back a glass of lemonade and some chips. Because studying in my room offers me two great advantages, I would say that my bedroom is my favorite place to study.

## B. Create new sentences using the expressions below.

(1) have a bone to pick with

_____

(2) make up with

_____

(3) come to terms with

_____

(4) break with

_____

## C. Find an error in each sentence.

(1) It takes several years developing good skill at skiing.

(2) I hate the thought to go back to the office where the boss is awaiting me.

(3) The apple juice is typical for this region.

(4) What is the matter for you?

## Q179. Explain about the one food you can't live without.

_____

_____

_____

_____

_____

### A. Sample Answer

This question makes me hungry just thinking of the one food I can't live without, which is any type of noodle. I love noodles of varieties. They can be spaghetti, rice, buckwheat, or even sweet potato noodles. Eating noodles is fun because you have to figure out how to pick them up with an eating utensil. Most people use forks, but in some countries they use chopsticks, which adds an even further challenge to this slippery food items. My favorite noodles are the clear sweet potato noodles that are made in Korea. They are sweet and very healthy. Also, I love that you can prepare the noodles in a variety of different ways. You can add tomato sauce, hot sauce, cheese sauce, and many other sauces. Because of this, I never get bored of eating noodles. Three hundred sixty five days a year I could eat a different type of noodle combined with a different type of sauce, and I'd never repeat it. Since I would never tire of eating noodles and they are fun to eat, I just couldn't survive without some form of noodles.

### B. Create new sentences using the expressions below.

(1) can't live without/can not do without

_____

(2) be immune to

_____

(3) get bored of

_____

(4) have a liking for

_____

### C. Find an error in each sentence.

(1) The country is seriously lacking at natural resources.

(2) We discussed about our holiday schedules.

(3) We took a long walk in snow.

(4) I decided to move out of the house on several reasons.

## Q180. What place has given you fond memories?

_____

_____

_____

_____

### A. Sample Answer

In my life, I have had many great memories. One of my fondest memories comes from my time in Germany. While I was there I was able to make great lasting memories and learn a few new things that would be of good use well into my adult years. To start with, I attended a German Preschool while I was there. Because of this, I was able to learn the German language as my first true spoken tongue. Up until I left for German, my parents had never heard me speak, so they always joke that German was my first language. Even more importantly, I learned about a new culture at a young age. Because of my exposure to other cultures, I have become a more tolerant person of others' own cultures. One of the most fun experiences while in Germany was what I call the Storyland Amusement Park; since then, I have forgotten its actual name. At this park there were different types of playground-like equipment that reenacted different parts of the famous nursery rhymes. The Little Old Lady Who Lived in a Shoe was my favorite, because you had to climb up this extremely high slide to the top of the shoe, and then you'd slide down through the shoe and out its foot! Germany gave me so many great memories!

### B. Create new sentences using the expressions below.

(1) make use of

_____

(2) make the most of

_____

(3) take advantage of

_____

(4) be tolerant to

_____

### C. Find an error in each sentence.

(1) She is married with a handsome youngman from Columbia.

(2) How long ago were you married?

(3) My sister was married five years ago and has two children.

(4) My younger sister is engaged with a bright young man.

## Q181. Describe a person with historical significance in your country. Explain the reason for his or her importance.

_____

_____

_____

_____

### A. Sample Answer

When asked to describe a person with historical significance in America, many would say Barrack Obama. However, I reject those opinions and would say President George Washington. First, he became the first president of the United States of America and was sworn into office on April 30th, 1789. As the first president, he set up many precedents that the following forty-three presidents would abide by. One of them is the basis of a two term presidency, which he did so by stepping down after serving two – four year terms. Another tradition that came about and shaped the American political world was the president's own choosing of his cabinet members. He also warned against foreign entanglements, which would help the succeeding presidents in running the newly found country. Because Washington worked off of merit and denied any royal treatment, all while successfully pulling an unstable country through some difficult times and setting up precedents in which our country still abides by, President George Washington is the most historically significant person in my country

### B. Create new sentences using the expressions below.

(1) set up

_____

(2) swear into office

_____

(3) value (ignore) tradition

_____

(4) cling to tradition

_____

### C. Find an error in each sentence.

(1) He warned us over the imminent dangers.
(2) The president set up many precedents for the citizens to keep by.
(3) George Washington is the most historical significant person in the country.
(4) He warned the people for foreign entanglements.

**Q182. What types of places, tropical, desert, rainforest, etc., would you like to go to spend a vacation?**

_____

_____

_____

_____

_____

## A. Sample Answer

Of all the types of places mentioned, I would be thrilled to go on a tropical vacation. This is mostly because I would be able to wear my favorite clothing type. I absolutely love wearing a swimsuit and skirt in the tropical weather. There's nothing like walking on a warm sandy beach with the warm sun on your skin and the cool ocean breeze blowing around you. Furthermore, when I go on vacation to a tropical environment, I would have a lot less to pack than if I went to let's say a Siberian climate. This is because I'd be outdoors most of the time, so all I would really need is some tank tops, shorts, skirts, flip-flops, and other basic necessities. I tend to over pack when I go anywhere, so this type of vacation would lessen my chances of doing this. Because I could wear my favorite clothing and I wouldn't have the need to lug around heavy luggage, I would chose to spend my vacation time in a tropical place.

## B. Create new sentences using the expressions below.

(1) There's nothing like ...

_____

(2) be thrilled to

_____

(3) bathe in the sun

_____

(4) lug around

_____

## C. Find an error in each sentence.

(1) My mother tends to take too many things with us when go a travel.

(2) The family went for a trip around the world.

(3) My family took a travel over the world last year.

(4) If giving a chance, I would choose to spend my vacation on the beach.

## Q183. Describe an activity that you and your family enjoy doing together.

_____

_____

_____

_____

_____

### A. Sample Answer

My family is a very geographically dispersed type family, so when we get together, we like to have fun. One way we do this is by going to the shore every summer. While we are at the shore, we go mini golfing. There are about 30 of us gathered all together; being my uncles, aunts, cousins, parents and siblings. We divide up into equal teams and take over the miniature golf course. Our favorite mini-golf location is a dinosaur one located in Naggs Head, North Carolina. My family is also highly competitive, but I don't follow in this suit. Because of this, we keep a careful eye on each other's teams to ensure that no one is cheating. Whoever is the losing team, they have to pay for everybody else's rounds of golf that day! My dad, older sister, younger brother and I are usually one team. Most of the time, we rank in the top three, so I love my team! Even though we are in heavy competition with each other, we still have an enjoyable time with each other while we are mini-golfing every summer at the beach.

### B. Create new sentences using the expressions below.

(1) follow suit

_____

(2) keep an eye on

_____

(3) be in heavy competition with

_____

(4) devide into

_____

### C. Find an error in each sentence.

(1) We are very competitive and keep eyes on each other.
(2) To ensure that no one is cheating, the inspector kept a careful eye on each testee.
(3) I took my picture with the White House in the background.
(4) Seeing from a distance the villa looked like a miniature castle.

## Q184. Who is the wisest person you know? What makes him/her so wise?

_____

_____

_____

_____

_____

### A. Sample Answer

My friend and immediate supervisor in the United States Army, CSM (Command Sergeant Major) Gabriel Arnold is the wisest person I have come to know. In the Army, we are to take orders from many different types of leaders. Often times, these leaders give their orders in a hurtful and blunt fashion. But, sometimes, we are lucky enough to be graced with the presence of a compassionate but firm leader. I was fortunate enough to have CSM Arnold as my leader, and at first I did not have a liking for him either. Later, my mind changed once I saw his leadership style and the way he gave great tough advice to me. Sometimes, the advice is not what we want to hear, but it is what we need to hear. He has experienced many things in life, which has brought him so much wisdom about how to treat others and the workings of life. Since this man has never lead me in the wrong direction when asked advice to and he leads people smartly, CSM Arnold is the wisest person I have encountered in my life.

### B. Create new sentences using the expressions below.

(1) come to know

_____

(2) take orders

_____

(3) be infamous for / be notorious for

_____

(4) enhance (lose) one's reputation

_____

### C. Find an error in each sentence.

(1) She is the most beautiful woman I ever met.

(2) His army experiences taught him with how to treat others.

(3) You will come across with a variety of people in your life.

(4) He looks fierce, but tender-hearted.

## Q185. What are more effective rewards, intrinsic rewards, such as praise, or extrinsic rewards, such as money?

_____
_____
_____
_____

### A. Sample Answer

As a student, I think that extrinsic rewards work the best for two reasons. To start with, I don't mind being bribed as a student to do my work well. If I do my work to the standards that are expected of me, getting a piece of candy or a gift card is a great motivator to me. One time, I worked really hard to become the number one student academically in my school, and I received two free tickets to the Spurs Jamboree! It was a great incentive to work even harder. Next, when other students see me getting all these rewards, they want to get them too. Therefore, they will work harder to try and beat me, which then in return I will do the same so that they can't beat me. Giving extrinsic rewards creates a friendly competition in the classroom that will bring about great results. So next time your teacher bribes you with a piece of candy or tickets to a show, focus on the task assigned to you and try to do your best to win that prize! You'll see how great it feels to be number one at something.

### B. Create new sentences using the expressions below.

(1) take a delight in / delight in

_____

(2) take ~apart

_____

(3) put ~together

_____

(4) be opposed to

_____

### C. Find an error in each sentence.

(1) Would you mind to open the window?

(2) Don't leave the baby cry alone in the cradle.

(3) Focus the task assigned to you.

(4) My little brother was well off to stay in the dormitory

## Q186. What custom or tradition that is unique to your country?

_____
_____
_____
_____

### A. Sample Answer

In America, we have two traditions or customs that are often practiced. The first tradition is tipping at a restaurant. When attending a restaurant in the USA, one must always tip their waiter. You should calculate at least 15% to 20% of the total bill as the tip to be given to your waiter. Also, we should almost always tip our taxi drivers, hotel cleaning staff, and bellboys. It is rather quite rude if you leave them empty handed for providing you a service. These types of jobs are often paid very little wages, so they rely on the tips as the majority of their income. Secondly, Americans celebrate Thanksgiving Day by having a huge feast of Turkey, vegetables, potatoes, and various pies. It is often celebrated with your entire family and is a whole day ordeal. It starts with the women cooking in the kitchen, the men watching the football game, and the children watching the Macy's Day Parade. While other countries might have some similarities to these traditions and customs, they are not the exact same as the American's way of tipping and celebrating what I have come to call Turkey Day.

### B. Create new sentences using the expressions below.

(1) take ~for granted

_____

(2) take heed

_____

(3) be similar to

_____

(4) be different from

_____

### C. Find an error in each sentence.

(1) Tom finished to work out at the gym and headed for his office.

(2) Take heed to not wake the sleeping baby.

(3) Despite of the doctor's efforts, the child died of pneumonia.

(4) They are not same as ours.

## Q187. Which person do you depend on for advice when dealing with a problem?

_____

_____

_____

_____

_____

### A. Sample Answer

The person whom I rely on for advice is my cousin, JJ. JJ is 10 years older than me and has been like a big sister to me my whole life. First off, since we have pretty much grown up around each other, she has seen me throughout my life and knows me pretty well. She knows what I would later regret doing or not doing. So she is great in that aspect! For example, one time, I wanted to take a dance class, but I was nervous about doing it. She told me to just do it because I would later regret not doing so. Secondly, she doesn't put her own opinions into her advice. She keeps it completely subjective. This is great because you don't want advice that is one sided. Also, she has traveled the world and experienced so much in life already. So, when I have a problem, I can always count on her to give me a fair and un-opinionated response.

### B. Create new sentences using the expressions below.

(1) grow up together

_____

(2) regret .... ing

_____

(3) suffer a nervous break-down

_____

(4) count on

_____

### C. Find an error in each sentence.

(1) Do you have anyone to rely on when you are in needs?
(2) Please count on me when you are in the trouble.
(3) He knew what I would regret to do later.
(4) He let the woman to cry herself out.

**Q188. Name a place that you have visited in your country that you would recommend to others to visit.**

_____
_____
_____
_____
_____

## A. Sample Answer

I would recommend everybody to visit the San Antonio, Texas River Walk. To begin with, San Antonio has a wealth of history and culture within its city limits. You can see the mariachi bands and singers performing, the bright colors of the Mexican culture that is very much a part of Texas, and the amazing food that has come to be known as Tex-Mex. It is the most delicious, flavorful, spicy food you well ever sink your teeth into. Also, the River Walk winds through the downtown area. Year round, you can take a tour on one of their river boats where a knowledgeable tour guide will tell you all about the history and hot spots to see. The best time to go is during the Christmas holiday season. In most other towns, parades are being held, and lights are being adorned onto homes. But, here in San Antonio, the boats and river is where the major happenings are. It is such a beautiful sight to see and the food is the added bonus to the River Walk in San Antonio, Texas.

## B. Create new sentences using the expressions below.

(1) due to / owing to / by dint of / thanks to

_____

(2) take possession of / be possessive of

_____

(3) are adorned (decorated) with

_____

(4) take lessons in~

_____

## C. Find an error in each sentence.

(1) What a beautiful sight they are!
(2) Cheer girls are dancing on the stage decorated on colorful flowers.
(3) The Moon Festival in Korea is very famous that even foreigners are looking forward to it.
(4) He was surprised with the eye-popping view.

## Q189. Of all the types of weather, rainy, sunny, snowy, etc., which is your favorite type of weather?

_____
_____
_____
_____
_____

### A. Sample Answer

Of all the mentioned types of weather, I'd have to say that snowy weather is my favorite type of weather. I have this opinion for two reasons that involve outside activities in the snow. First, after it has snowed, I can go outside and make a snowman! I love using old scarves, and other old items to build with. One year, I made snowman using broom sticks, an old electric cable, and soda bottle tops. It was definitely a very strange looking man, but it was still a lot of fun to construct it outside in the snow. Next, I love to snowboard! There is something exhilarating about rushing down a steep slope with the cold wind and warm sun in my face. I've been snowboarding since I was old enough to walk, so as soon as that first snow happens, I'm ready and waiting for the ski resorts to open! Because I am able to do two of my favorite outdoor activities during this type of weather, I really adore the snow.

### B. Create new sentences using the expressions below.

(1) consist of

_____

(2) be composed of / be made up of

_____

(3) achieve one's end/ attain one's object

_____

(4) be determinded to

_____

### C. Find an error in each sentence.

(1) She is old enough getting married
(2) The snow is enough deep for the children to snowboard upon.
(3) I made a snowman with using a broomstick.
(4) I made a snowman similar in shape with my brother.

**Q190. If you're given a month of leisure to do whatever you'd like to do, what would you do in that month?**

_____

_____

_____

_____

_____

## A. Sample Answer

If I had a whole entire month of leisure time, I'd do two things that I just never have the time to do in my real life. First, I'd travel back to the USA and visit all of my family. I haven't seen most of them in three years! So, it would be great to see how much the children have grown, and to catch up with the life happenings of those loved ones. It would take me three weeks to travel all over the USA to where my family is dispersed about. Then, I'd use my last week of free time to go on a vacation to somewhere tropical. I love hot weather, so I'd probably wind up in Thailand. A week isn't enough time to see everything over there, but at least it's a start. The first thing I'd do there is to enjoy the food and get a ride on an elephant. I'd close out my Thai trip by visiting some of the Buddhist temples that are well-known in those parts of the world. I just can't fathom having a whole month of leisure time, but if I did, I'd go visit my family whom I haven't seen in what seems like forever, and I'd travel a bit in Thailand.

## B. Create new sentences using the expressions below.

(1) have enough time

_____

(2) catch up with

_____

(3) keep up with

_____

(4) fall behind one's schedule

_____

## C. Find an error in each sentence.

(1) I haven't seen you since I had left the town.

(2) I will be back by ten minutes.

(3) I want to catch up with time I have spent uselessly.

(4) The first thing I want to do there is visting my friends.

## Q191. What is your most memorable moment that you have experienced in school?

_____

_____

_____

_____

_____

### A. Sample Answer

The most memorable moment that I had experience in school was the time that I had to do a school project in my Theology class at Allentown Central Catholic High School. This project was developed to try and give just a small sense of understand to how much work and effort it takes to having a family, getting married, and maintaining a house. At the time, I had a huge crush on a boy, Peter, who was in my Theology class. Well, lucky me, he became my partner in this project, and were married, only in the class project's eyes, and not in real life, unfortunately. It was very memorable, because I found out that he had liked me too during this process. I had to meet and interview his parents, and he had to do the same to mine. We also had to go shopping for wedding rings, dresses, and venues. Then report all of our research back in a portfolio. The buying a house portion was the most fun, because my cousin was a realtor, so we go to actually experience the real process. Having been married to my crush before we had ever even dated is something that I will never forget! How could I?

### B. Create new sentences using the expressions below.

(1) take time to

_____

(2) maintain a house

_____

(3) the most memorable moment in one's life

_____

(4) go shopping for

_____

### C. Find an error in each sentence.

(1) What is most memorable experience in your life?

(2) What is wrong for you?

(3) He lacks of common sense.

(4) My car is running out gas. We have to find a gas station.

## Q192. Compare the advantages of positive rewards against the advantages of negative punishments.

_____
_____
_____
_____
_____

### A. Sample Answer

When thinking about positive rewards versus negative punishments, one must think of all the advantages and disadvantages. I will discuss predominately the advantages of each. For the positive rewards' advantages, there is the feeling proud of oneself to begin with. When you receive a gift, such as a gift card or money, you will feel happy inside. Also, positive rewards will bring about repeat actions of the same behavior, because you will want to obtain that same benefit again. As for the advantages of negative punishments, one main one comes to my mind. It is that if we punish undesirable behavior, then that behavior will be known to the doer, and will eventually stop. For example, if I am at home and I never clean my room, my mom will threaten me to take away my TV. When I failed to clean my room, away went my TV for a week. I was angry, but it worked! I always clean my room now for fear that I will lose my TV again. As I mentioned previously, there are advantages to rewarding somebody for good deeds, but there are also advantages for punishing those who do bad things.

### B. Create new sentences using the expressions below.

(1) feel proud of

_____

(2) figure out

_____

(3) for fear that + clause

_____

(4) reward one for

_____

### C. Find an error in each sentence.

(1) As soon as she got well, she goes to visit her parents.

(2) His father was much healthier than was expected.

(3) I never expected to see you here, Mary.

(4) He was very lazy that he wouldn't move even his finger to clearn the room.

## Q193. If a close friend was in need of an organ, such as a kidney, and you were a viable option, would you give them the organ needed?

### A. Sample Answer

Without skipping a beat, I would absolutely give an organ to a close friend if I were a viable option. I would do this for two reasons. First, I wouldn't want to see my close friend die. If they are considered to be my close friend, then that means they are very important to me. What fun would life be, if they died from kidney failure? Who would I go to the movies with and laugh at the bad acting with? Who would I go out on midnight runs to get some ice cream at the convenience store with? It just wouldn't be the same. The second reason is that I would be overcome by a huge rush of guilt that would last for the rest of my life. I only regret one thing in my life that happened years ago. I still have not let go of that guilt. Therefore, if I didn't give my viable organ to my close friend, then I'd be in reality, the one killing them. I just couldn't live a happy life knowing that I could have prevented their death by doing something about it.

### B. Create new sentences using the expressions below.

(1) let go of

_____

(2) lead a happy life

_____

(3) could have + pp

_____

(4) must have + pp

_____

### C. Find an error in each sentence.

(1) A friend in need is indeed, went a saying.

(2) One of my uncles died with a kidney failure.

(3) He is in the hospital with a breaking leg.

(4) You will be happy if you let go away all the worldly desires.

## Q194. What would you like to know if you could learn one thing about the future?

_____

_____

_____

_____

_____

### A. Sample Answer

The one thing I've always wanted to know about the future is if I will eventually become rich. I don't want to learn about my death, or who I'll marry, because those things are a natural part of life. By learning about the fact that I will be rich or not, it will help me to accept my fate in the financial world at an earlier time. Then, I could set realistic goals of my own financial status now, because I know that eventually, I will come into a great deal of money, or not. This futuristic knowledge would come into great use, especially when buying a house, paying for college, or investing in some stocks. I could know to put a little or a lot aside, because I would know how much money I'll need to live in the future. Also, it will alleviate some of the burdens I have now. One of my biggest I have is worrying about how to support my family. If I know that I will be financially secure in the future, I'll be more comfortable and my mind will be more at ease with raising my children in a good living environment.

### B. Create new sentences using the expressions below.

(1) come into use

_____

(2) be at ease

_____

(3) worry about

_____

(4) be contended with / be content with

_____

### C. Find an error in each sentence.

(1) Who is in charge to support your family?

(2) He is responsible to the task.

(3) It is necessary to see where the responsibility lays.

(4) In trying to matter English, you cannot afford neglecting daily study.

## Q195. Describe a peculiar dream of yours.

_____

_____

_____

_____

### A. Sample Answer

I often have strange dreams, but the most peculiar one that I've had occurred just last night. My mom always warned me about eating sweets before going to bed, and I've always abided by these rules. However, last night, I had not just a small bowl of ice cream, but a huge bowl of ice cream. This induced a strange dream, just like my mother said it would. My dream went something like this. I was walking along the street, when all of a sudden a flock of flying monkeys was seen in the sky. I quickly ran into a nearby store where to my surprise, there was a herd of hopping kangaroos trying to escape! If this wasn't already the strangest dream I had ever had, it got even more bizarre. One of the kangaroos scooped me up and put me into their pouch. We hopped along the streets until we met a swarm of slithering snakes who then took me as their prisoner. I thought one of them was going to eat me, but they just wanted to lift me up into the trees and let me swing on them! As I was swinging from one snake to the next, like Tarzan, the snakes disappeared, and I started falling. Then I woke up. I don't think I will ever eat ice cream at night before bed again!

### B. Create new sentences using the expressions below.

(1) escape from

_____

(2) all of a sudden / out of blue

_____

(3) have a sound sleep

_____

(4) suffer from insomnia

_____

### C. Find an error in each sentence.

(1) I am troubled from insomnia.

(2) The fire fighters came to the rescue when I was on the verge of death.

(3) He sat in until late at night studying for the final exam.

(4) The snakes were disappeared when mom shook me out of the nightmare.

## Q196. Describe what you would miss from your home if you went abroad to study.

_____

_____

_____

_____

_____

### A. Sample Answer

There are two things that I would greatly miss from my home if I went abroad to study. I would miss my friends first and foremost. My friends mean the world to me and it just wouldn't be the same without them. Although this may be true, I know I would make many new friends at my school in a foreign country. Then, maybe, one day, my friends that I've had since I was a child and the ones that I would make in my new temporary home could meet. Then, all of my friends could make even more friends. Besides my friends, I would miss my pet lizard, Louie. I know that I wouldn't be able to take him with me, so he would have to stay behind in my home country. Often times, Louie and I curl up together and take a nap. Yes, he is a lizard but he acts just like a cat! Being in a new country to study would be an amazing experience, but I'd still miss my friends and Louie, my pet lizard.

### B. Create new sentences using the expressions below.

(1) go abroad to study / go study abroad

_____

(2) make friends with

_____

(3) become homesick

_____

(4) after ten years of absence

_____

### C. Find an error in each sentence.

(1) He made friend with many boys and girls while traveling overseas.

(2) We changed bus at the next stop and continued our trip.

(3) Your scissor is not good enough to cut the cloth.

(4) I bought new shoes at the shoes store on the corner.

## Q197. Do you prefer to relax or to do another activity when you are taking a break from studying?

_____

_____

_____

_____

### A. Sample Answer

I would prefer to relax when taking a break from my studies. First of all, there have been studies done that prove that by doing less you are actually doing more. Furthermore, by taking naps or breaks away from the office your productivity and performance will be boosted. How so you might ask? It's because we just don't have enough time to do everything we want. So, then we overload our plates and try to cram it all in at once. We might start off doing pretty well, but by the end of the day, we've burnt all of our energy. As a result, our work has become less efficient, which requires more time later to fix. If we would take a short break, then we could recharge our batteries and get back to work more refreshed. On the contrary, if I would do another activity, like going on a bike ride, I'd feel even more tired, which is counter-productive to my work load. All in all, taking a break completely from studying will benefit you more than if you went out and did something else during your break from hitting the books.

### B. Create new sentences using the expressions below.

(1) make contributions to

_____

(2) serve the purpose of

_____

(3) be instrumental in

_____

(4) think to the contrary

_____

### C. Find an error in each sentence.

(1) Taking breaks from time to time will improve your production.
(2) It is wise for you to save for a rainy day.
(3) It is foolish you to cram all the materials at once without taking a break.
(4) It is recommended that you took a break from time to time.

## Q198. Do you prefer learning about movies before you see them or not knowing anything about them and being surprised?

_____

_____

_____

_____

### A. Sample Answer

I am a huge movie buff! So, to me I will enjoy a movie either way. However, if I had a preference, it would be to learn about the movie before seeing it. From time to time, I watch a movie and I'm in complete disappointment from it. So by learning about a movie before seeing it, I could prevent my let-down from taking place. Knowing what the movie is about will give me a realistic expectation, instead of some grandiose idea of what I think it should be about. Presently, I've been interested in seeing action romance movies. Because of this, I like to know about the movie a little bit so I can better understand the dynamic story that will unfold before me. Having just a hairline of a clue about the movie will ease my mind's confusion of who is who, and who loves who. I'm not saying I want to know how the movie will end, but just the basics of who the characters are and what their back stories are. All things considered, I enjoy just a tidbit of knowledge before watching a movie, for the purpose of being more prepared for the event of a let-down and to help make a mental map of the characters in the story.

### B. Create new sentences using the expressions below.

(1) be inferred from

_____

(2) on board

_____

(3) adjust to

_____

(4) adapt oneself to

_____

### C. Find an error in each sentence.

(1) Even a slight clue about the story will greatly help understood the movie.

(2) "Don't let me down, little gentleman!" His father encouraged the boy to work hardly.

(3) Just as men are fond of sports, like women are fonding of chatting.

(4) Frankly spoken, he is a liar.

## Q199. What must be considered when choosing a job or career?

_____

_____

_____

_____

_____

### A. Sample Answer

When people are choosing their job or career, they must consider two very important factors. The first is whether or not they will be able to perform in that job or career. Imagine that you strongly dislike children or can't stand the sight of blood, then choosing a job that relates with the youth of the world or medical care would be the wrong move on your part. Therefore, you should make a list of the things you are willing to do and not willing to do. Then use that list to make a judgment on the appropriate path. The second important factor to be considered when choosing a job or career is the skills or talents you possess. Say that you are a computer whiz or a mathematical genius, then fields related to those special abilities would suit you perfectly. Why not chose a job that comes naturally to you, rather than a job that you will struggle to understand? By thinking of your abilities, both your talents and your drawbacks, you will be able to make a fitting decision in selecting your future job or career.

### B. Create new sentences using the expressions below.

(1) stand (=endure)

_____

(2) take effect (=go into effect)

_____

(3) devote one's life

_____

(4) go bad / turn sour

_____

### C. Find an error in each sentence.

(1) When people are choosing his job, they must consider two things first.
(2) Take a list of jobs you want to work.
(3) Then across out the items that appeal you least one by one.
(4) Let me know that you are coming.

## Q200. If you had the opportunity to learn a musical instrument, what would you learn?

_____

_____

_____

_____

_____

_____

### A. Sample Answer

Given the opportunity to learn a musical instrument, I would learn the piano. To begin with, my mother plays the piano. She would be able to give me lessons for free! It would be a great mother-daughter bonding activity and she would be very happy if I showed interest in one of her passions. We could even learn how to play duets! Furthermore, all of my favorite bands incorporate the piano into their music. If I learned piano, I could learn how to play all of my favorite songs! I think it would be quite soothing to sit down and play a song or two from my favorite band. So, because I could spend more time with my mom and learn how to play songs from my favorite bands, I would like to learn how to play the piano.

### B. Create new sentences using the expressions below.

(1) intend to

_____

(2) for free

_____

(3) interest someone in

_____

(4) in that + clause

_____

### C. Find an error in each sentence.

(1) She knows how to deal in the musical instrument to produce beautiful sounds.

(2) I spent a lot of time with my sister to play hide and seek.

(3) "Excuse me, ma'am. My intentions are good", said the boy.

(4) I think it would be quite soothing sitting down together and play some notes.

## Q201. Describe an experience of going on a picnic with your school.

_____

_____

_____

_____

_____

### A. Sample Answer

The best experience I've ever had was going on a picnic with my school when I was in fifth grade. To start off, the weather was absolutely perfect that day. Every other year my class had gone on a picnic, it had always been rainy and windy. We thought it was a curse! However, on the day of my 5th grade picnic, the sun was shining brightly and there was a cool breeze. It was nice enjoying the sunshine rather than being stuck underneath the picnic shelter to avoid the rain. Another reason the picnic was so much fun was because that was the year my team won the baseball game. Every year at the picnic, there was a baseball game. This was the first time I had ever been on the winning team. I even got a home run! I didn't hit the ball very hard, but I was fast enough to get to home plate before anyone could stop me. Due to not only having the perfect weather conditions, but winning the baseball tournament as well, the best experience I ever had at a picnic was when I was in 5th grade.

### B. Create new sentences using the expressions below.

(1) not sleep a wink

_____

(2) be sold out

_____

(3) take notice of

_____

(4) tag along

_____

### C. Find an error in each sentence.

(1) This was the first time for me to be in the winning team.
(2) No body could stop me reaching the home plate.
(3) I got a head trick in the soccer game and voted the MVP.
(4) The well-wishers came by two and three.

## Q202. Describe how you dress. Why do you dress this way?

_____

_____

_____

_____

_____

### A. Sample Answer

I have to admit that I was blessed with a very good sense of fashion. Whenever I pick out clothes to wear, I keep two things in mind. The first thing I remember is that one should always dress to impress. While I am only a college student, I believe it is best to always dress as nicely as possible. You never know who you might run into! Many students go to class in sweat pants, flip flops, and a sweatshirt. However, in today's looks-based society, you will be judged on what you look like. You need to leave a good impression! Another important consideration I have is that I want to express myself through my clothing. For this reason, I like to pick out interesting pieces to suit my uniqueness. For example, I love wearing strange jewelry. My favorite piece is probably my necklace made of silver ware. It's a great conversation starter. To conclude, whenever I go shopping, I always like to pick out clothes that look nice and adequately express my personality.

### B. Create new sentences using the expressions below.

(1) be blessed with

_____

(2) keep .... in mind

_____

(3) express oneself

_____

(4) pick out

_____

### C. Find an error in each sentence.

(1) Mom told me to keep what she said in my mind.

(2) She is very clever that she always picks out perfect clothes to suit her uniqueness.

(3) The dress looks good for you.

(4) You look so great with the pink dress.

## Q203. Describe your favorite holiday. Why is it your favorite holiday?

_____

_____

_____

_____

_____

### A. Sample Answer

Of the many holidays my country has, I believe that Independence Day is my favorite. First of all, Independence Day always falls during the summer time. This means that all of my friends are home from school. My best friends and I unfortunately attend different universities. It's not very often that we have time off together during holidays. However, Independence Day is one that we can all spend together. To continue, Independence Day is a day filled with many exciting activities! My family and I always start off the day watching my little brother play with his high school band in the annual parade. After that, we go down to the beach and have a barbecue with our friends and family. We play lots of games, like volleyball and badminton. We end the night watching the spectacular fireworks display over the lake. Every year it seems to get better and better! To sum up, I love Independence Day because I get to do many fun activities with my best friends and family.

### B. Create new sentences using the expressions below.

(1) have time off

_____

(2) be filled with

_____

(3) to sum up

_____

(4) have one's own way

_____

### C. Find an error in each sentence.

(1) What holidays celebrated in your country?
(2) Thanksgiving Day marks on the third Thursday in November.
(3) Today checks the tenth anniversary of the school foundation.
(4) How many red-lettered days do you have in your country?

**Q204. Describe how you learn a foreign language. Why do you learn this way and is it the best way for you to learn?**

_____
_____
_____
_____
_____
_____
_____
_____

## A. Sample Answer

The most efficient way for me to learn a foreign language is to find a friend who is a native speaker of the language. For example, when I was learning Spanish, my friend Juanita invited me over to her house often. I was introduced to delicious Mexican cuisine, new music, and TV shows. Moreover,  She also corrected my pronunciation and taught me slang words that you wouldn't be able to find in a Spanish textbook. When I studied abroad in Mexico, I was able to sound like a native speaker. Some people even asked me where I was from because I had a really good Spanish accent. Therefore, I think it's best to learn a language by finding a buddy who is a native speaker of the language you want to learn.

## B. Create new sentences using the expressions below.

(1) apologize to ~ for  ~

_____

(2) be indulged in

_____

(3) abandon oneself to

_____

(4) be addicted to

_____

## C. Find an error in each sentence.

(1) He speaks English in heavy Korean accents.

(2) He has a good command in English.

(3) I was surprised at the fluency in which he spoke Spanish.

(4) What is your mother's tongue?

## Q205. Describe your favorite sport.

_____

_____

_____

_____

_____

### A. Sample Answer

Though many foolish people don't consider it a sport, my favorite sport is cheerleading. To begin with, cheerleading is quite physically demanding. It requires weight training as we have to be able to lift each other as well as toss each other up in the air. We also have to work on our cardio. Cheerleading is a very high energy sport that requires a lot of jumping around. Furthermore, cheerleading requires a strong bond between the members of the squad. As I mentioned earlier, cheerleaders have to lift each other up in the air and do many stunts that are quite dangerous. Our communication skills and timing have to be perfect in order to perform a perfectly executed stunt. I feel that the bond I have with my cheerleading friends is much stronger than the bond I have with others. In conclusion, due to its demands, cheerleading is my favorite sport.

### B. Create new sentences using the expressions below.

(1) delve into

_____

(2) descend from

_____

(3) deserve well of (cf. deserve ill of)

_____

(4) be destined to

_____

### C. Find an error in each sentence.

(1) He regards the book the best of its kind.

(2) He referred to the island the flower of the Pacific.

(3) The bond I have with my close friends is very strong that nothing can breaks it.

(4) My uncle was used to lift me up in the air when I was a little girl.

## Q206. What is the most important subject you study at school?

_____
_____
_____
_____
_____
_____

### A. Sample Answer

Though I study many necessary subjects at school, I think that the most important subject is English. To start off, English is an extremely popular language. Many people all over the world learn English. So, even if you travel to a country where you don't know the language, there is a good chance you'll still be able to communicate with people if you know English. There always seems to be someone everywhere that knows the language. You don't need to learn many different languages as long as you know English. Secondly, in my English class, we read many interesting novels. These novels help to mold my world perspective. I have learned many valuable lessons from books such as The Scarlet Letter, 1984, and Great Expectations. I love reading and examining the author's critique of the world. It enables me to remain sensitive to, yet critical of, the world in which I am growing up. Thus, I believe English is probably the most important subject that I learn in school.

### B. Create new sentences using the expressions below.

(1) major in

_____

(2) a required subject (an elective subject)

_____

(3) complete the required course.

_____

(4) enable one (something) to V

_____

### C. Find an error in each sentence.

(1) Reading books will surely broaden your perspective for the world.

(2) A widely read person is more likely having deeper insight into human nature.

(3) My sister was majored in the Russian Language and Literature.

(4) I lost an interest in literature. In my graduate course, I took engineering at my major.

## Q207. What has been your most important academic achievement?

_____

_____

_____

_____

_____

### A. Sample Answer

To this day, my most important academic achievement was when I got a higher grade than my brother in our chemistry class. In the first place, my brother is known as "the smart one." He always gets perfect grades in everything! He isn't modest about his intelligence, either. Every chance he gets he likes to remind me of how well he is doing in all of his classes. So, getting a higher grade than him, even though it was only one point higher, gave me something to annoy him with. Additionally, the sciences have never really been my strong subject. Science just didn't really interest me. Also, science deals with a lot of numbers. I tend to do poorly in anything that even slightly resembles math. However, having my twin brother in my chemistry class pushed me to try my hardest. By beating him in chemistry, I proved not only to him, but also to myself, that I am intelligent too. Because I was able to silence both my brother's disparaging remarks about my intelligence as well as my own, getting a higher score in my chemistry class than my brother was my crowning academic achievement.

### B. Create new sentences using the expressions below.

(1) be modest about

_____

(2) in retrospect

_____

(3) A resembles B

_____

(4) gain good results

_____

### C. Find an error in each sentence.

(1) Chinese Literature he took as his minor was interested him more and more.

(2) He later became a Chinese major on graduate school.

(3) He finally got a Ph.D for Chinese literature.

(4) Now he is one of the prominent professors on the field.

## Q208. What type of music do you like the most?

_____
_____
_____
_____
_____
_____

### A. Sample Answer

My favorite type of music is anything calming with inspiring lyrics. The first reason I like this type of music is because I am the type of person that gets stressed out very easily. I am very busy and always trying to do everything perfectly. I very rarely get a moment to relax and constantly feel tense. When I do relax, I want to listen to mellow music that will alleviate my stress. By listening to peaceful music, I can take a momentary escape from my hectic life. Another important aspect I consider when choosing music is the lyrics. I want to be uplifted by my music. I don't want to listen to music filled with negative words and depressing lyrics. I need something that will remind me that the world is a beautiful place and even when things do go wrong, the resulting problems won't last forever. Listening to motivational lyrics is like being serenaded with a pep talk! Therefore, I love listening to motivational music that soothes me.

### B. Create new sentences using the expressions below.

(1) feel tense/get stressed out

_____

(2) do things perfectly

_____

(3) alleviate/soothe/calm down

_____

(4) be uplifted by

_____

### C. Find an error in each sentence.

(1) He was elated for success.

(2) The boy came home in high spirits as he got a perfect score for the English test.

(3) I used to referred to the cramming method to get higher marks.

(4) He stayed up until late night studying for the final exam.

## Q209. What expectations do you have of your parents?

_____
_____
_____
_____
_____
_____
_____

### A. Sample Answer

I believe there are two basic expectations that parents need to meet. The first is that parents need to let their children make mistakes. Parents will do their children a disservice is they never allow them to do foolish things that will teach them lessons. For example, I once dated a boy that my parents hated! Despite their feelings towards him, they let me continue to date him until he ended up breaking my heart. They were then there to comfort me and talk to me about what happened. I learned a lesson I will never forget and I appreciate that my parents let me make that mistake. Another requirement parents must fulfill is to give their child the basics such as food, water, and shelter. Every child needs those to grow up to be strong healthy. Children don't necessarily have the means to provide those for themselves, so parents need to make sure that they fulfill those basic needs. So, every parent should allow their children to make mistakes as well as provide them with the basic necessities for survival.

### B. Create new sentences using the expressions below.

(1) meet the expectations

_____

(2) provide one with

_____

(3) meet halfway (=negotiage, compromise)

_____

(4) minor in (cf. major in)

_____

### C. Find an error in each sentence.

(1) I appreciate you for the help.

(2) I think him being a good friend.

(3) I am grateful you for your kindness.

(4) He didn't come to work due with a sprained ankle.

## Q210. What would wish for if you had one wish?

_____
_____
_____
_____
_____

### A. Sample Answer

If I had one wish, I would wish for a time machine. First of all, as far as I know, a time machine has yet to be invented. Think of how much money I could make by letting scientists examine my time machine in order to build a duplicate! With all of this money, I could pay off my student loan debts, send my parents on a relaxing vacation, and buy a nice house away from the public eye. I would also donate a lot of it in order to better the quality of life of many others. Additionally, if I had a time machine, I could go back and observe the past. I would love to know what life was really like in the past. For example, I could find out if my dad was really as popular as he insists that he was. With careful research, I could also pinpoint what exactly caused the extinction of the dinosaurs. It would also be nice to relive some of the happiest moments of my life all over again. Because I could make a lot of money and experience the past, I would wish for a time machine if I were given one wish.

### B. Create new sentences using the expressions below.

(1) come true

_____

(2) fulfill one's wish

_____

(3) call for

_____

(4) behind schedule/ ahead of schedule

_____

### C. Find an error in each sentence.

(1) I hope your wish come true.

(2) I wish I am rich!

(3) The flood came on as a result of heavy rains.

(4) "Blessed are those who are poor in the mind." says the Bible.

**Q211. Some parents give their children money on a monthly basis. At what age should children receive an allowance and how much should they receive?**

_____

_____

_____

_____

_____

**A. Sample Answer**

As I have never received one, I do not believe children should receive an allowance. The first reason I don't believe children should receive an allowance is because they need to learn to work for their money. If a child needs money, he should earn it, not receive it for free. I had to get a job when I was young so that I could start paying for my own things. For example, I watched the neighbors' dogs while they were out of town or pulled weeds out of their gardens. When I was old enough, I got a real job. Another reason I think children should not receive an allowance is because they will most likely use it to purchase wasteful things. Children typically don't do anything that would require an allowance. So, they would probably spend their money on candy or toys that they don't need. Parents don't need to pay for their children to indulge their every desire. Although my point of view may seem a bit harsh, I believe parents don't need to give their children an allowance.

**B. Create new sentences using the expressions below**

(1) free of charge

_____

(2) get above oneself (=think highly of oneself)

_____

(3) spoil somebody

_____

(4) get a reputation as (for)

_____

**C. Find an error in each sentence.**

(1) He wasted money for trifling things.
(2) It is wise for you to get ready in advance.
(3) Most Korean parents give allowance to their sons and daughters by they get a job.
(4) The youngesters should be trained to cope for the difficulties in this global era.

## Q212. Who do you like the better, athletes or entertainers?

_____

_____

_____

_____

_____

_____

### A. Sample Answer

Although I love both, I think athletes are better. To start off, athletes tend to be better role models. Today, many entertainers are involved in all kinds of scandals. Movies these days are filled with inappropriate content, song lyrics are more often than not very offensive, and the clothing entertainers wear leaves little to the imagination. Though athletes aren't completely scandal-free, they seem to make better decisions than many entertainers these days. The second reason I like athletes better is because they teach us to respect our bodies. They must keep their bodies in amazing condition. However, unlike many entertainers, they don't achieve this goal through crazy fad diets or skipping meals. Instead, they eat healthy, get plenty of rest, and exercise. I believe many of us would be much better off if we had the dedication of athletes. To conclude, because athletes seem to be more respectable, I prefer athletes to entertainers.

### B. Create new sentences using the expressions below.

(1) tend to

_____

(2) are involved in

_____

(3) filled with

_____

(4) be better off / be badly off

_____

### C. Find an error in each sentence.

(1) The song lyrics were so offensive that I turned on the music.

(2) I prefer beating the drums to watch others playing the instruments.

(3) Mr. Kim is endowed on linguistic talent.

(4) Great athletes are usually spoken highly and enjoy great popularity.

## Q213. Describe your most unforgettable day. Why will you never forget this day

_____

_____

_____

_____

_____

### A. Sample Answer

My most unforgettable day was my very first day of high school. The first reason this day is unforgettable to me was because I found out that I had a peanut allergy that day. During lunch time, I sat with my new friends and began eating my peanut butter and jelly sandwich. Soon, I noticed that my throat was closing up and I couldn't breathe. Luckily, someone called the school nurse and she injected me with some liquid that saved me from suffocating. It was quite a harrowing experience. Moreover, thanks to my lunch time scare, I was given a nickname that day that followed me throughout the rest of my high school days. I went to my last class of the day. Some kid from the cafeteria recognized me and asked me if I was that "peanut butter girl" that almost died in the cafeteria. From that day forward, I was called "peanut butter girl", "peanut butter", or simply "PB." My friends still call me one of those names to this day. In summary, thanks to my peanut butter and jelly sandwich, my first day of high school remains my most unforgettable day.

### B. Create new sentences using the expressions below.

(1) unforgettable day (experience, etc.)

_____

(2) be sensitive to (be allergic to)

_____

(3) come to help (resque)

_____

(4) out of reach

_____

### C. Find an error in each sentence.

(1) Thanking to the unusual incident, I still remember the day as the most unforgettable one.
(2) The church remained to be intact in the fierce bombing.
(3) One's medicine can be another's poison, tells an old saying.
(4) He was denied with access to the children.

## Q214. Who will you remember the most after you finish school, your friends or your teachers?

_____
_____
_____
_____
_____
_____

### A. Sample Answer

After I finish school, I will remember my friends more than my teachers. To begin, I had a variety of teachers over my school years. All of them were wonderful and did leave some kind of impression on me. However, I had one close group of friends from elementary school all the way through high school. They were there in some of my happiest and saddest days. I have learned some much about them I feel like they are practically family. I could never forget my two best friends. Additionally, my friends and I have created some pretty amazing memories together. For example, I will never forget the time we stayed up all night at the lake. One of my friends had just found out her parents were getting a divorce. We got into her car and drove until we were too tired to continue. We put blankets down on the sand, ate junk food, and talked until she felt better. We did end up getting in big trouble, but that is still one of the fondest memories I have. So, while I did have many great teachers, I will never be able to forget the times I spent with my best friends from school

### B. Create new sentences using the expressions below.

(1) a variety of

_____

(2) leave impression on

_____

(3) be engaged to

_____

(4) read between the lines

_____

### C. Find an error in each sentence.

(1) I will be never able to forget the time I spent with Jane.

(2) Summer vacation starts at June.

(3) Koreans cannot live off kimchi.

(4) After lunch, they cleared up the area.

## Q215. Describe your idea of a happy life.

_____

_____

_____

_____

_____

### A. Sample Answer

I believe that there are two elements necessary to having a happy life. First of all, people spent a majority of their life working. It would be depressing to dread going into work every day. To be truly happy, I think one needs to enjoy his job. Getting stuck in a job you don't like means you will be constantly stressed and cranky. For example, I once worked at McDonald's and I hated that job. Every day before I went into work I was filled with dread and every day after work, I was exhausted and in a terrible mood. Secondly, having a loving family is absolutely necessary. Everybody needs someone who will be there for them no matter what. When you are having an off day, you need a family member there to cheer you up again. Engaging in conversation and bonding with others is a sure fire way to keep your spirits high. I know that whenever I'm having a bad day, talking to my sister always makes me feel better. To sum up, a happy life doesn't require much, just a job that you enjoy going to and a family that loves and supports you.

### B. Create new sentences using the expressions below.

(1) reaction with (somebody)

_____

(2) reckon without

_____

(3) be reduced to

_____

(4) keep one's spirit high

_____

### C. Find an error in each sentence.

(1) Psy became popular since that time.

(2) He was sorry at his making the mistake

(3) He was absent at school last Monday.

(4) I came to school on bike.

## Q216. Which genre of books do you enjoy reading the most? Why?

_____
_____
_____
_____
_____
_____

### A. Sample Answer

As an avid reader, I love many books, but my favorite genre of books is probably the "How-to" genre. To start off, these books are filled with an immense amount of knowledge pertaining to a wide variety of subjects. There are how-to books for every topic imaginable, from how to change a light bulb to how to make people like you. As I am living on my own now, I use these books to teach me how to make delicious meals, fix broken things, and do my taxes. Another benefit of reading how-to books is that they are a great way to make friends and keep friends. If you know how to do a bunch of different things, you'll be a big help to others who don't have those skills. My friends call me all the time to help them change their oil, mend their clothing, or teach them how to speak Russian. All of these skills I learned myself through how-to books. I'm now able to pass my knowledge on to others! Due to the benefits reading books from this genre, the "How-to" genre is my absolute favorite!

### B. Create new sentences using the expressions below.

(1) get down to (=start)

_____

(2) get even with (=revenge)

_____

(3) stand at advantage

_____

(4) get in touch with (=communicate with)

_____

### C. Find an error in each sentence.

(1) He had walked out when I had a chance to explain.
(2) He is an expert in the Korean history.
(3) I often watch the famous singer at TV.
(4) I usually go to bed lately on weekends.

## Q217. Which fruit do you like the most? Why?

_____

_____

_____

_____

_____

### A. Sample Answer

Though I don't care much for fruit, there is one fruit that I adore—the strawberry. First of all, strawberries are a delicious fruit that you can use in many recipes. While I have to admit that I enjoy plain strawberries the best, strawberry pie is also extremely tasty. They're also perfect in salads, chicken, or cakes. One of my favorite drinks at Starbucks is the strawberry lemonade that they serve in the summer time. Moreover, strawberries can make anything unhealthy seem instantly healthy. For example, whenever I eat a bowl of ice cream, my mother always tells me I'm going to get fat. One day, I decided to put strawberries atop my ice cream. When my mom walked by this time, she told me she was proud of me for trying to eat healthier. So, adding strawberries to unhealthy food help to disguise the fact that you're eating so poorly. To conclude, I think strawberries are the best fruit because they're not only delicious and versatile, but also give off the illusion you are eating healthier.

### B. Create new sentences using the expressions below.

(1) care for

_____

(2) a special recipe

_____

(3) get fat/lean

_____

(4) be on a strict diet

_____

### C. Find an error in each sentence.

(1) I am sorry to have kept you waited.
(2) Mom, I'll live up at your expectations.
(3) I am opposed to children to stay up too late.
(4) The family was well off to do business in the new country.

## Q218. What is your favorite TV show and why?

_____

_____

_____

_____

_____

### A. Sample Answer

My favorite TV show is Modern Family, a show about three different American families. The first reason I like the show so much is because it represents the changing family dynamic in the United States. While one stereotypical American family is included, there is also a family consisting of an older man with a divorced young Colombian wife and a family made up of two gay men and their adopted Asian daughter. America is changing and this show does a good job of reflecting that change. Furthermore, the show is funny. All day long I have to deal with stressful people and things. When I go home at night, I don't want to watch dramas with even more stressful people and things. I want to laugh. Modern Family makes me laugh out loud through the majority of the episode due to the witty one-liners and the ridiculous messes that the characters get themselves in that I can relate to. Because the show is a good reflection of American society and also very comical, Modern Family is my favorite TV show.

### B. Create new sentences using the expressions below.

(1) be worthy of

_____

(2) go berserk

_____

(3) all the rage

_____

(4) go rampant

_____

### C. Find an error in each sentence.

(1) The painter drew the pictures not in a brush, but with his fingers.

(2) The lines of his poems were usually written in the pencil.

(3) Some parts of the poem were written in the red.

(4) We traveled over the desert in airplane.

## Q219. What is your favorite movie and why?

_____

_____

_____

_____

_____

### A. Sample Answer

My favorite movie is a recent one, the Perks of Being a Wallflower. Firstly, the main actor of the movie, Logan Lerman, is a phenomenal actor and attractive. Everything about his persona is perfect for the role he is playing. He recites his lines with the perfect amount of awkwardness and craziness that the role calls for. His facial expressions also match the caliber of his voice. They're subtle yet powerful at the same time. The fact that he is handsome only adds to his appeal in the movie. Secondly, the movie does a pretty good job of describing what life in high school is like. No matter what he did, Logan Lerman just couldn't fit in with the majority of the high school population. However, he does find some pretty amazing friends that have his back throughout the entire film. He deals with a variety of typical high school situations, like dating, parties, football games, and heartache. It also addresses some sensitive topics in a very mature manner. So, I would recommend the Perks of Being a Wallflower due to the superb acting of Logan Lerman and the content of the film.

### B. Create new sentences using the expressions below.

(1) be immuersed (lost, engrossed) in

_____

(2) play the role

_____

(3) act as

_____

(4) person to person

_____

### C. Find an error in each sentence.

(1) He was incapable to walk up the staircase.

(2) I met James Bond person in person at Hollywood.

(3) It took ten years for the staff to finish the new version with huge amount of money.

(4) However, it was not much sucessful as the old edition.

## Q220. Compare the advantages and the disadvantages of Smart Phones.

_____
_____
_____
_____
_____

### A. Sample Answer

Smart Phones are all the rage all over the world. Though there are many advantages to smart phones, there are also a number of disadvantages as well. The first main advantage of Smart Phones is the fact that you can access the internet using them. This is an awesome feature that helps you stay connected with your friends and family. For example, you can send emails, messages on Facebook, and even use video chatting to stay in contact with all of your friends. It's also a great tool if you happen to get lost often, as most have some kind of GPS system. However, with the unlimited access to the internet comes a major problem—it's extremely easy to get carried away with your cell phone use. How many times have you gone into a coffee shop and seen friends simply playing on their cell phones instead of having a conversation? I once had a boyfriend that used his cell phone all the time instead of talking to me. It made me feel really unimportant and I eventually broke up with him because of it. To conclude, Smart Phones can be awesome, but we need to make sure not to get too carried away with them.

### B. Create new sentences using the expressions below.

(1) steal the show

_____

(2) beside oneself

_____

(3) in search of

_____

(4) be adept at ~ing

_____

### C. Find an error in each sentence.

(1) She almost broke out with him because of his rudeness.

(2) "You'd better not to go." said her mother.

(3) He knew immediately that the question was beside his capability.

(4) How can I figure up the secret of the universe?

## Q221. Which option is healthier, eating three large meals a day or eating four to five small meals a day?

_____

_____

_____

_____

_____

### A. Sample Answer

It is much healthier to eat three large meals a day instead of several smaller meals. First of all, eating three large meals is just as effective at keeping your body full and satiated as eating several small meals. If you eat enough at breakfast, your body most likely won't be hungry until lunch time anyway. You don't need several small meals throughout the day to keep your hunger levels down. As I don't get hungry very often, eating four to five small meals a day would be too much for me. To continue, I simply don't have the time or capability of eating four to five small meals a day. I work full-time in a setting that doesn't permit several breaks for eating meals. I have time for breakfast in the morning, lunch during my lunch break, and then dinner when I get home. It would be inconvenient for me to rearrange my schedule in order to accommodate four to five small meals a day. The added stress from doing that would just lead to poorer health. Thus, I think it's healthier for me to stick to my three-meal schedule.

### B. Create new sentences using the expressions below.

(1) be accustomed to / get used to

_____

(2) be apt to

_____

(3) stand to reason (=make sense)

_____

(4) be strange to (= strange to / new to)

_____

### C. Find an error in each sentence.

(1) Do you believe the phrase, 'Habit is a second nature.'? Yes, I believe.
(2) He has been trying to get rid his stuttering habits.
(3) The added stress would be led to poor health.
(4) It is really hard to stick on your first plan.

## Q222. If you could win a lot of money, how much would you want to win and why?

_____
_____
_____
_____
_____

### A. Sample Answer

If I won the lottery, I would want to win one million dollars. The first reason is because lottery winnings get taxed. I want to win enough money so that I can still pay off my debts after much of the cash is lost to taxes. I owe money to many people. For example, I owe money to many of my friends who lent me money to buy an iPad, iPod, Macbook, and iPhone 5. I also owe my parents who paid to fix my car after I hit a mailbox and dented the front of it. Lastly, I owe money to the government because they loaned me money for college. Secondly, I think one million dollars is sufficient for my needs. My money management skills aren't the best yet. I feel that if I won a lot more than that, I would waste money on frivolous things that I don't want or need. Plus, I want to be able to use up all of my winnings fairly quickly so I don't have a long line of people at my door asking me to lend them money. I just want enough to pay off my debts. After all, money is the root of all evil. So, if I won the lottery, I think winning one million dollars would be perfect.

### B. Create new sentences using the expressions below.

(1) be exempted from

_____

(2) duty-free shop

_____

(3) owe A to B

_____

(4) be sufficient for

_____

### C. Find an error in each sentence.

(1) If I won the lottery, I will donate most of the money to the charity.

(2) The lottery winner spent all the money and finished up empty-handed.

(3) He had enough money to pay for all his debts.

(4) Ten million dollars are good enough to help the poor people in my village.

**Q223. We are continuously learning and doing new things in life and often times we fail at our first attempt. Describe your first attempt to gain something new.**

_____

_____

_____

_____

## A. Sample Answer

My first attempt to learn how to mow the yard was an absolute disaster, much to the chagrin of my lawn-savvy father. The first thing that went wrong when I was mowing the yard was that I didn't mow it in the right pattern. My dad had mentioned something about mowing the yard in a certain pattern, but I wasn't really listening. So, when he went to mow the backyard and left me up front, I mowed the grass as I saw fit. Unfortunately, my dad was quite upset when he came up to inspect my work. I was mowing the grass in the wrong direction. Apparently, this hurts the grass. To continue, I destroyed my mom's rosebush. While mowing, I saw my cute neighbor running by. I lost focus on mowing and accidentally mowed over my mother's beloved rosebush. When my mom saw her mutilated rosebush, she looked as if she wanted to cry. I felt terrible. To sum up, although mowing the lawn turned out terribly, there was a bright side—my dad never asked me to help out with yard work again.

## B. Create new sentences using the expressions below.

(1) fail in one's attempt

_____

(2) go wrong (badly)

_____

(3) be upset

_____

(4) fall a pray to

_____

## C. Find an error in each sentence.

(1) I lost focus at mowing the grass.

(2) My dad has never asked me to mow the grass from then.

(3) The yard work turned out terribly.

(4) While he was living, the poet was not appreciated very much.

## Q224. Describe your ideal holiday resort.

_____

_____

_____

_____

_____

_____

### A. Sample Answer

There are two things that would make any holiday resort perfect. First of all, the holiday resort should have an unlimited amount of food available at all hours. The food should include a wide variety of meats, cheeses, chocolates, ice cream, and baked goods. When you're on a holiday, you should be able to eat whatever you want whenever you want it with minimal work involved. We should only worry about eating healthy in our normal day-to-day lives. Holidays are a chance to indulge. Moreover, every resort needs a king-size waterbed in every room. My neighbor used to have a waterbed, and it was the most comfortable bed I have ever laid on. At home, I have a very uncomfortable mattress. When I go on a holiday, I want to drift off to sleep on a cloud, which is basically what a waterbed feels like. Plus, they are fun to jump around on. To conclude, in order for a holiday resort to be considered ideal, it should have an unlimited 24-hour buffet as well as a waterbed in every room.

### B. Create new sentences using the expressions below.

(1) make something perfect

_____

(2) a wide variety of

_____

(3) worry about

_____

(4) be familiar with (cf. be familiar to)

_____

### C. Find an error in each sentence.

(1) I has met him by this time yesterday.

(2) I rained during several days.

(3) My family took a trip of Hawaii.

(4) We used to play soccer in Saturdays.

## Q225. What is your biggest ambition in life?

_____

_____

_____

_____

_____

_____

### A. Sample Answer

My biggest ambition in life is to travel to every single country on the planet. The first reason this is my biggest ambition is because it seems almost impossible to do; after all, there about 200 countries in the world. As an American, it will be hard for me to even get into some countries, such as Cuba and North Korea. The price of traveling all over the world is a bit daunting as well. Traveling to every country would be extremely difficult. Another reason that is my biggest ambition is because I want to experience the cuisine of several different countries. I am an aspiring chef and I want to learn all of the tips and secrets about cooking. There's also got to be some rare ingredients hidden away in this great big world that would take the taste of my food to the next level. I could create amazing dishes that America has never seen the likes of if I could experience food from every country on the Earth. So, currently, my biggest ambition in life is to travel to every country in the world.

### B. Create new sentences using the expressions below.

(1) be ambitionus of

_____

(2) seems to –V

_____

(3) all ~have to do is

_____

(4) pay lip service

_____

### C. Find an error in each sentence.

(1) He left to his home country last week.

(2) The plane is bound to Seoul, Korea.

(3) The hardest thing to learn is being a good loser.

(4) She is good for singing.

## Q226. Which person or teacher influenced you the most? Why is this person a positive role model?

_____
_____
_____
_____
_____

### A. Sample Answer

The person that has influenced me the most would have to be my brother. One of the reasons he has influenced me so much is because he was my best friend growing up. My brother was my constant companion. He was always up for a game of soccer or monopoly. Even when we grew up and went to college, my brother was still always there looking out for me. He helped me pass my chemistry class and let me hang out with his friends when I was struggling to make friends of my own. Additionally, my brother is one of the most caring people I have ever met. He always listens to my problems, no matter how futile or girly they might seem. He also spends much of his free time helping others. Whenever his friends need help, he's always there for them, whether it be taking their dog for a walk or giving them a ride at three in the morning. He's currently studying medicine so that he can make a profession of his love for helping people. To sum up, my brother has influenced me the most of anyone I have ever met. I hope to be as good as him someday.

### B. Create new sentences using the expressions below.

(1) have an influence on

_____

(2) take account of

_____

(3) when it comes to ~ing

_____

(4) correspond to

_____

### C. Find an error in each sentence.

(1) They made friend with each other.

(2) My little brother is curious on the stars at night.

(3) We are fully ready to take care for the matter.

(4) Smoking does us more harm than good.

## Q227. Where do you see yourself in twenty years?

### A. Sample Answer

Though 20 years seems like a really long time away, I know what I want to have achieved by then. First, I want to be living in Africa. I recently read a book about a woman who started a hospital in Africa for poor African women. Though her life seems quite difficult, it also seems very fulfilling. I am currently studying medicine at my local university and I want to use the skills I'm learning there to better the lives of many neglected African woman. So, I want to be in Africa in 20 years. Furthermore, I hope to have a family. More specifically, I want a husband, a daughter, and a dog. My whole life I have wanted to be a mother and raise a child to be globally aware. My daughter will be able to help me out in my hospital and see that life isn't about money and tangible objects. I want a dog because I absolutely love dogs and couldn't imagine my life without one. Also, I want a husband to support my ambitions and give me chocolates on Valentine's Day. To conclude, in 20 years I see myself in Africa with my small, but perfect, family.

### B. Create new sentences using the expressions below.

(1) keep abreast of (=stay level with)

_____

(2) keep a straight face

_____

(3) keep company with

_____

(4) keep faith with

_____

### C. Find an error in each sentence.

(1) I have no concern in that sort of thing.
(2) You should have been studied harder.
(3) How about to go biking this afternoon?
(4) He is right at home for the piano.

## Q228. What quality or qualities do you look for in a best friend?

_____
_____
_____
_____
_____
_____
_____
_____

### A. Sample Answer

All of my best friends share two specific qualities, so those must be the qualities I look for in a best friend. One quality I think is important is athleticism. I am a very active individual. I love sports, hiking, and simply being outside. I would want my best friend to engage in those activities with me. It would be hard to connect with someone who had no interest doing the things I spend a majority of my free time doing. To continue, I want my best friend to be smart. I like talk about global issues; they're something I'm passionate about. I want my best friend to be able to talk to me about those things and have the conversation actually be intellectually stimulating. Also, I want to be able to learn new things from my friends. It would be boring to have a friend who couldn't intellectually challenge me. Thus, I think it is important for my best friends to be athletic and intelligent.

### B. Create new sentences using the expressions below.

(1) share A with B

_____

(2) engage in

_____

(3) be passionate about

_____

(4) be boring

_____

### C. Find an error in each sentence.

(1) That man is the taller of them all.

(2) Marathon is one of the harder sport games.

(3) Brown is the brightest than any other in the class.

(4) Whoever who wins the race will get this gold ring.

**Q229. Parents should be required to pay for their children's university education. Do you agree or disagree with this statement?**

_____

_____

_____

_____

## A. Sample Answer

I wholeheartedly disagree that parents should have to pay for their child's university education. To begin with, college is expensive! The worst part is that college costs continue to increase. College is a huge investment nowadays and it's not fair to expect parents to shoulder that burden. Children need to pay at least a portion of that cost by getting a part-time job or taking out loans that they will pay back. Parents have already spent a considerable amount of money on their children. Another reason parents shouldn't be expected to pay for college is because students might slack off if they're not responsible for paying for it. There are a lot of non-academic distractions in college. It would be very easy to skip class if the student isn't really being held accountable for it. However, if the student is paying, he will know the true cost of every class and will be much more apt to go to class. Failing a class would be much more painful if the student realizes that he has to pay again for a class he has already taken once. So, I think it is best if parents are not required to pay for their child's tuition.

## B. Create new sentences using the expressions below.

(1) be required to

_____

(2) get mad at (with)

_____

(3) not care much for

_____

(4) a compaign to

_____

## C. Find an error in each sentence.

(1) Would you mind to lend me ten pounds?
(2) Good pronounciation is not above anyone
(3) You are to be blamed.
(4) English is called as the universal language.

## Q230. Describe the qualities of a good citizen?

_____
_____
_____
_____
_____

### A. Sample Answer

In order to be considered a good citizen, I believe an individual must possess two qualities. To start off, a good citizen is one who abides by the laws. Laws were created in order to ensure social harmony. If someone goes around violating the laws, he is showing that he has no respect for the well-being of himself, other citizens, or his country. However, if you abide by the laws, you are showing you care about your country and those in it. Secondly, a good citizen will vote. Voting is such an important part of ensuring the continued success of a nation. By voting, a citizen is showing that he does care about the fate of his country. A nation can only grow if citizens are actively involved in that growth by choosing the people and the laws that will govern the country. To sum up, if citizens are law-abiding and take the time to vote, I believe they possess the qualities it takes to be good citizens.

### B. Create new sentences using the expressions below.

(1) give an account of

_____

(2) have good taste in

_____

(3) Chances are that~ may~

_____

(4) There is a chance that

_____

### C. Find an error in each sentence.

(1) Citizens participate in the government administration with casting votes.
(2) Some citizens were deprived with their suffrage.
(3) Most citizens voted with human rights activists.
(4) The Royalists were defeated for the general election.

## Q231. What are the most important qualities of a good teacher ?

_____

_____

_____

_____

_____

### A. Sample Answer

I believe there are two important qualities that every good teacher possesses. The very first of those is patience. In today's society, is seems like students are continually becoming more disrespectful towards the teachers. A good teacher is aware of this and will try to be as patient as possible with the students. If a teacher blew up each time a student did something disrespectful, nothing would ever get done in the classroom. This also would not be good for the teacher's health. A good teacher needs the patience to let some things slide while addressing other situations as calmly as possible. A second important quality a teacher should possess is the capability of relating to his students. Teachers have the task of teaching difficult concepts to students. The easiest way for students to grasp these concepts is by getting examples that they can understand. If a teacher can explain things using pop culture references or simpler terms, the students will be able to better comprehend what is being taught to them. To sum up, in order for a teacher to be successful, he must be patient and able to relate to his students.

### B. Create new sentences using the expressions below.

(1) blame one for ~ing

_____

(2) drop by / stop by / drop in at, etc.

_____

(3) open an account with (a bank)

_____

(4) declare for customs

_____

### C. Find an error in each sentence.

(1) We have to discuss about our holiday plans.

(2) He is clever, but he is lacking of experience.

(3) Would you like to go on a swim?

(4) We awaited for the train for two hours.

## Q232. What qualities does a good student have to have?

_____

_____

_____

_____

_____

### A. Sample Answer

Every good student should take responsibility for himself as well as have a good imagination. Firstly, many students think that it solely the teacher's responsibility to help them succeed. However, this is not the case. A student needs to be responsible for his own academic career. This includes asking for help when it is needed, completing all assigned tasks, and studying the material given to him. A student needs to be an active participant in his own education. He cannot depend on others to make him academically successful. Additionally, a good student needs a good imagination. I believe imagination and creativity are often over looked in today's modern education system. Imagination allows students to ask questions that will further their understanding of the material. It also gives them an advantage by allowing them to think outside of the box and come up with new approaches to solving seemingly difficult problems. Without an imagination, a student will miss out on many academic opportunities. Therefore, I think that taking responsibility for one's learning as well as having an imagination are qualities every student should possess.

### B. Create new sentences using the expressions below.

(1) leave no stone unturned

_____

(2) leave (the result) to chance

_____

(3) come up with

_____

(4) let alone (=not to mention, not to speak of)

_____

### C. Find an error in each sentence.

(1) Please fill in the form with ink.
(2) You are required to fill up the form with black.
(3) Math is something I have a lot of difficulty in.
(4) She likes being looked in.

113

## Q233. What would you change about your country if you were given the opportunity?

_____
_____
_____
_____
_____

### A. Sample Answer

If given the opportunity, I would like to change my country's past. To start off, my country was deeply involved in the slave trade not too long ago. This is one of the things I am most ashamed of about my country. Not only did we profit off of the slavery of an entire race of people, but we treated them terribly as well. We denied them basic human rights and beat them horribly. Many slaves were malnourished, overworked, and treated like animals. Just thinking about it sickens me. Furthermore, I would like to change my country's response to immigration during World War II. In an attempt to keep America prosperous, my nation rejected several refugees seeking shelter. What's even worse is that most of those refugees were facing persecution in their own countries that ultimately resulted in death. If I could go back in time, I would have the United States take all of those people in with open arms. So, although it's not possible, I would greatly appreciate the opportunity to change my country's

### B. Create new sentences using the expressions below.

(1) be ashamed of

_____

(2) deny A B

_____

(3) be entitled to

_____

(4) appreciate something

_____

### C. Find an error in each sentence.

(1) Refugees ultimately ended off in death.
(2) I am ashamed of my country which cruelly traded with slaves several decades ago.
(3) I am looking forward to a visit at my hometown.
(4) Looking back on it, I wish we didn't given in so earily.

**Q234. Do you agree with the following statement? An eye for an eye. Why or why not?**

_____

_____

_____

_____

_____

### A. Sample Answer

Although "an eye for an eye" may seem like an appealing approach, I don't think it is a practical philosophy. First of all, as another old saying explains, two wrongs don't make a right. No matter what anyone does to you, you should not retaliate in the same manner. The satisfaction you may temporarily feel will soon dissipate and you will most likely feel bad about your childish behavior. It is better to take alternative steps to solving your problem rather than retaliating in the same way in which you were wronged. To continue, no one is ever justified in directly bringing harm onto someone. It is not your decision to say whether or not the other person suffers. The justice you seek for an act done against you should always include a third party. That third party will have an unbiased approach and invoke the appropriate solution to the issue. You don't have the authority to directly harm any other being. Thus, I disagree with the statement "an eye for an eye."

### B. Create new sentences using the expressions below.

(1) would rather (not)

_____

(2) do a good job

_____

(3) put an end to

_____

(4) take the subway to

_____

### C. Find an error in each sentence.

(1) He lives next door to mine.

(2) He was blamed by his sister to be absent from the meeting.

(3) I took a trip on the world.

(4) Do you remember the boy I was going out?

## Q235. What is the most important job or task you have ever had? Why was it important?

_____

_____

_____

_____

_____

### A. Sample Answer

The most important job I have ever had was babysitting when I was in high school. To begin with, babysitting requires a huge amount of skill. First of all, you need to know how to change diapers. This is a smelly, yet necessary, task. You also have to be able to cook meals and not burn down the house in the process. Lastly, you have to keep the children entertained so that they don't turn on you and refuse to cooperate with you. Another reason why it is important is because a child's life is in your hands. You have to constantly stay alert. The parents entrusted you with their child's life. That's a pretty big deal. You can't be lazy and text on your cell phone while the child wanders off on his own. You must be diligent and engaged. If you mess up, you could severely endanger the life of the child. That's not a mistake you can simply erase and do over again. Therefore, I believe that the most important job I have had was when I was a baby sitter in high school.

### B. Create new sentences using the expressions below.

(1) be prerequite to

_____

(2) rise in the world

_____

(3) entrust A with B

_____

(4) take the place of

_____

### C. Find an error in each sentence.

(1) What time he was coming did he say?

(2) Why are you so happy about?

(3) It is a boring place to live!

(4) Do you think who is the brightest boy?

## Q236. What are the advantages and disadvantages of studying abroad?

_____

_____

_____

_____

_____

### A. Sample Answer

Studying abroad is an exciting yet difficult adventure. To begin, I think one of the best things that comes from studying abroad is the experience of meeting and interacting with new people. I once studied abroad in France. I met so many wonderful people from all over the world. They taught me their ways of life and culture. I even dated a French student from the university I attended. I still remain close friends with him and the other friends I made. However, there is one huge disadvantage of studying abroad—culture shock. Culture shock is when you are extremely frustrated by the differences between your culture and a foreign culture. For example, when I traveled to Mexico, the men liked to whistle at girls. I hated being whistled at. It was also difficult to get used to the laid back lifestyle of Mexicans. They didn't seem to care about time and my Mexican friends often showed up late when I made plans with them. While I think the advantages of studying abroad far outnumber the disadvantages, one should still be a bit cautious about studying in a foreign country.

### B. Create new sentences using the expressions below.

(1) be liable for (=be responsible for)

_____

(2) be liable to (=be apt to, be inclined to)

_____

(3) be likely to

_____

(4) find fault with

_____

### C. Find an error in each sentence.

(1) Johnson insisted that he took the responsibility of carrying all the luggage.

(2) The teacher recommended that the youngsters stayed behind the experienced students.

(3) The officer insisted that his men followed his order all at once.

(4) The leader ordered that all the members followed his directions.

## Q237. Describe your dream job. Why is it your dream job?

_____

_____

_____

_____

_____

_____

### A. Sample Answer

My dream job is to become a talk show host. There are two reasons I would love to be a talk show host in the future. Firstly, if I were a talk show host, I could meet many famous people. I would make sure to interview everyone from celebrities, to scientists, to humanitarians. After the show, I would invite them over to my house for dinner. Then, I could ask all the questions I couldn't on the show, see what they're really like off camera, and maybe we could become good friends. Moreover, I have pretty good people skills. The reason for this is because I worked at McDonald's for about 4 years while in high school. At this job, I had to interact with all different kinds of personalities. As I was in a professional setting, I didn't have the option of ignoring or yelling at people I didn't like. I had to learn how to cope with different people, even people that I hated. In conclusion, because I would like to become friends with influential people and because I don't want my awesome people skills to go to waste, my dream job is to host my own talk show.

### B. Create new sentences using the expressions below.

(1) get together with

_____

(2) suit one's taste

_____

(3) to cope with

_____

(4) run a business

_____

### C. Find an error in each sentence.

(1) He knows how to cope with all the problems raising by the labor union.

(2) How was the weather like?

(3) I wasn't aware of that it was so late.

(4) Juliet found herself was in love with Romeo.

## Q238. At what age is it appropriate to allow a child to stay home alone?

_____

_____

_____

_____

_____

### A. Sample Answer

From my experience, I think the best age to allow a child to stay home alone is thirteen. To begin with, at this age, a child has all of the basic skills and knowledge to be safe while at home. For example, by thirteen, I mastered how to feed myself, take care of my personal hygiene without any help, and keep the house safe from intruders. I also knew all of the basic information that might be helpful in an emergency, like my address, where my parents worked, and their phone numbers, among other things. Secondly, leaving a child who is under thirteen home alone would look bad if something bad did happen. By this, I mean that if something happened and people found out that you left a child home alone, you would look like a bad parent. Though a child might have the basic skills required to be safe at home at a younger age, accidents do happen all the time. Leaving a teenager at home alone doesn't sound as scandalous as leaving a child home alone. Those are the two reasons why I think thirteen is a good age to leave a child home alone.

### B. Create new sentences using the expressions below.

(1) much less / much more

_____

(2) by the time

_____

(3) in proportion to

_____

(4) originate in

_____

### C. Find an error in each sentence.

(1) Don't leave a baby alone in the room. Keep eyes on it all the time.

(2) I asked that she was unhappy about her marriage.

(3) I want something to write. My pen is out of ink.

(4) Many impotant discoveries have been made by accidents.

**Q239. Some people say that the quality of a product is more important. Others say that the price of a product is more important. Which statement do you agree with and why?**

_____

_____

_____

_____

_____

## A. Sample Answer

I think the quality of a product is much more important than the price of that product. Firstly, you won't have to repurchase a quality product often. For example, I once purchased a laptop computer simply because it was cheaper. Unfortunately, the quality of the product was as cheap as the price. Within a few months, I had to purchase a new computer due to issues with my cheap one. I would have saved myself lots of money had I simply purchased the higher quality computer in the first place. Furthermore, prices can be deceiving. I have a friend who purchased expensive makeup that ended up performing worse on her skin than a drugstore brand. She should have done her research and not simply let the price of the makeup persuade her to purchase it. To conclude, choosing a product based on quality versus price is the only way to ensure your satisfaction.

## B. Create new sentences using the expressions below.

(1) be in inverse proportion to

_____

(2) have trouble with

_____

(3) persuade ~ to

_____

(4) listen to reson (=listen to and think about good advice)

_____

## C. Find an error in each sentence.

(1) Choosing a prodect basing on its quality is natural.
(2) How long did it take you collecting so many stamps?
(3) I'm not a professional. I play violin for fun.
(4) Do you have any sepcial interests beside your job?

## Q240. How will you help a foreigner learn about your country?

_____

_____

_____

_____

### A. Sample Answer

The best way to teach a foreigner about my country, the United States of America, is to introduce him to my culture. There are two ways I could do this. The first way is to take him to important tourist locations. One important place I would undoubtedly take my friend is New York City. NYC represents the diversity of my country the best. There are many different types of cultures thriving in the city, so my friend could understand the importance of diversity in the United States. Another good way to introduce a foreigner to my country is to watch many movies with him. Films give a fairly accurate representation of the cultural ideals of the United States. For example, the movie Remember the Titans shows the after effects of slavery in the States as well as the southern football culture. Another important movie for him to see would be The Godfather. This film portrays the gangsterism of America's past and how immigration has impacted American society. Both movies show elements of the United States that I wouldn't necessarily be able to give my friend an experience of first hand. Thus, in order to help a foreigner learn about my country, I would take him to tourist locations such as NYC and watch movies with him.

### B. Create new sentences using the expressions below.

(1) without the fatigue of

_____

(2) be caught in the act

_____

(3) do away with

_____

(4) practice law / priactice medicine

_____

### C. Find an error in each sentence.

(1) Did you say that ten days were required to complete the work?

(2) The longer we study, the tireder we get.

(3) comparing to the others, they are the two best boys on the team.

(4) "Will you do it again, Jim?" " Never I will do it, mon."

# Answers for Section C. Find an error in each sentence.

121. (1) At Christmas ->On Christmas

(2) to play hide and seek-> playing hide and seek

(3) for each other->at each other

(4) to play in the snow-> playing in the snow

122. (1) you as well as I am -> you was well as I are

(2) his moral views at -> his moral views on

(3) as much as -> as long as

(4) and you will -> or you will be

123. (1) at my first visit-> on my first visit

(2) all more nervous ->all the more nervous

(3) to visit-> visiting

(4) in a trouble ->in trouble

124. (1) are required to have -> is required to have

(2) the Christianity -> Christianity

(3) Considered -> Considering

(4) with hunger -> of hunger

125. (1) with no avail -> to no avail

(2) one's view on life -> one's view of life

(3) outlook for life -> outlook on

(4) satisfied for - >satisfied with

126. (1) I think students should not work.... -> I don't; think students should work ....

(2) unable studying -> unable to study

(3) me working -> me to work

(4) deprives him from his liberty -> deprives him of his liberty

127. (1) are not enough -> is not enough

(2) Atmosphere -> The atmosphere

(3) to discuss about the pollution -> to discuss the pollution

(4) heavily fined -> was heavily fined

# Answers for Section C. Find an error in each sentence.

128. (1) <u>on the child</u> -> to the child

(2) <u>in the public</u> -> in public

(3) <u>deals with</u> -> deals in

(4) <u>a lot times</u> -> a lot of time

129. (1) <u>showed</u> -> showing

(2) <u>for valuable opinions</u> -> with valuable opinions

(3) <u>discuss about my future major</u>-> discussed my future major

(4) <u>to abide with</u> -> to abide by

130. (1) <u>get health</u> -> get healthy

(2) <u>from  Latin</u> -> in Latin

(3) <u>to ride itself of toxic materials</u> -> rid itself of toxic materials

(4) <u>without sleeping well</u> -> without having slept well

131. (1) <u>something to you</u> -> something for you

(2) <u>is studying hard</u> -> studying hard

(3) <u>worth of $1,000</u> -> worth $1,000

(4) <u>worthy praise</u> -> worthy of praise

132. (1) <u>idea</u> -> ideas

(2) <u>Welcome to home</u>-> Welcome home

(3) <u>takes note</u> -> takes notes

(4)  no error

133. (1) <u>weight</u> ->weigh

(2) <u>stay you healthy</u> ->keep you healthy

(3) <u>more sleeping</u> -> more sleep

(4) <u>in a good health</u> -> in good health

134. (1) no error

(2) <u>tends to</u> -> tend to

(3) <u>in a tense relation</u> -> in a tense relationship

(4) <u>Most of people</u> -> Most of the people

# Answers for Section C. Find an error in each sentence.

135. (1) to be please -> to please

(2) to solve the problem -> solving the problem

(3) to draw a conclusion -> drawing a conclusion

(4) to dance and sing -> dancing and singing

136. (1) makes fun at -> makes fun of

(2) was jeered by -> was jeered at by

(3) no error

(4) An old saying went -> An old saying goes

137. (1) with a bank -> in a bank

(2) robbed money from the bank -> robbed the bank of money

(3) with their leaves -> of their leaves

(4) robbed money of a bank -> robbled a bank of money

138. (1) every other days -> every other day

(2) for chores around the house -> with chores around the house

(3) busy to attend ->  busy attending

(4) with doing his homework-> with his homework or doing his homework

139. (1) interested for -> interested in

(2) good for-> good at

(3) in mathematic -> in mathematics

(4) envious in -> envious of

140. (1) too many cookers -> too many cooks

(2) no error

(3) participating with -> participated by

(4) came up on -> came up with

141. (1) most important -> the most important

(2) having a stranger -> to have a stranger

(3) likened to travel -> likened to traveling

(4) Few student is -> Few students are

# Answers for Section C. Find an error in each sentence.

142. (1) <u>from malnutrition</u> -> of malnutrition

(2) <u>went out</u> -> was gone off

(3) <u>thought him</u> -> thought of him

(4) <u>thought of him</u> -> thought him

143. (1) <u>to laugh happily</u>-> laugh happily

(2) <u>was elected as the president of</u> -> was elected the president of

(3) <u>on the next Sunday</u> -> for the next Sunday

(4) <u>are required for attendance</u> -> are ruquired to attend

144. (1) <u>turn around to my mom</u> -> turn to my mom

(2) <u>without any fail</u> -> without fail

(3) <u>to talk freely</u> -> to talk with freely

(4) <u>relieved from worries</u> -> relieved of worries

145. (1) <u>to borrow money</u> -> to lend money

(2) <u>could have bought a ferrari</u> -> could buy a ferrari

(3) <u>on the 10<sup>th</sup> street</u> -> on 10<sup>th</sup> street

(4) <u>on the vacation</u> -> on vacation

146. (1) <u>becoming wth</u> -> becoming to

(2) <u>goes on</u> -> goes with

(3) <u>not worthy the price</u> -> not worth the price

(4) <u>try in</u> -> try on

147. (1) <u>to me to get together</u> -> for me to get together

(2) <u>He was used to work out</u> -> He used to work out

(3) <u>is the one of the best ways</u> -> is one of the best ways

(4) <u>dangerous more than</u> -> more dangerous than

148. (1) <u>could pass</u> -> could have passed

(2) <u>could have beaten</u> -> could beat

(3) <u>sick in the bed</u> -> sick in bed

(4) <u>Everybody is envious for</u> -> Everybody is envious of

# Answers for Section C. Find an error in each sentence.

149. (1) to take -> to bring

(2) bring this book -> take this book

(3) came in the last -> came in last

(4) came in the second -> came in second


150. (1) the movie -> the movies

(2) enjoy wonderful dinner -> enjoy a wonderful dinner

(3) stay there late at night -> stay until late at night

(4) in study of -> in the study of


151. (1) also but -> but also

(2) established herself for -> established herself as

(3) famous for -> famous as

(4) is well known as -> well known for


152. (1) passed -> passing

(2) driving a car -> to drive a car

(3) Have it not been for you -> Had it not been for you

(4) to answer the questions -> answering the questions


153. (1) grown up ->grew up

(2) was elected as the President of ->elected the President of

(3) White House ->the White House

(4) as his ->for his


154. (1) are forcing -> are forced

(2) to find -> find or in finding

(3) Finished-> Finishing

(4) need -> needs


155. (1) for better -> for the better

(2) live up for -> live up to

(3) Thanks for -> Thanks to

(4) a renting house -> a rented house

# Answers for Section C. Find an error in each sentence.

156. (1) <u>knocking the door</u> -> knocking at the door

(2) <u>contact with me</u> -> contact me

(3) <u>I have played</u> -> have I played

(4) <u>Rarely he plays</u> -> Rareply does he play

157. (1) <u>while I had a shower</u> -> while I was having a shower

(2) <u>my preference taste</u> -> my preference

(3) <u>best</u> -> most

(4) <u>The chapter 10</u> -> Chapter Ten / The 10th chapter

158. (1) <u>build up a vacabulary</u> ->build up vacabulary

(2) <u>the dictionary</u> -> in the dictionary

(3) <u>comes with</u> -> comes up with

(4) <u>much sense</u> -> any sense

159. (1) <u>on stage</u> -> on the stage

(2) <u>try eating</u> -> try to eat

(3) <u>in our team</u> -> on our team

(4) <u>in the committee</u> -> on the committee

160. (1) <u>fighting</u> -> to fight

(2) <u>ring truly</u> -> ring true

(3) <u>in 1950's</u> -> in the 1950's

(4) <u>who is he</u> ->who he is

161. (1) <u>ten years before</u> -> ten years ago

(2) <u>two years ago</u> -> two years before

(3) <u>didn't see</u> -> haven't seen

(4) <u>Who is do you think...</u> -> Who do you think is ...

162. (1) <u>tell a truth</u> -> tell the truth

(2) <u>telling the lie</u> -> telling a lie

(3) <u>went</u> -> goes (runs)

(4) <u>will return</u> -> will be rewarded

# Answers for Section C. Find an error in each sentence.

163. (1) <u>I don't too</u> -> I don't either

(2) <u>had better to hurry up</u> -> had better hurry up

(3) <u>What's happen?</u> -> What happened?

(4) <u>I had a trouble moving this heavy bag</u> -> had trouble

164. (1) <u>Most of students</u> -> Most students/Most of the students

(2) <u>nor he like</u> -> nor he likes

(3) <u>gave a birth</u> -> gave birth

(4) <u>have headache</u> -> have a headache

165. (1) <u>in pronouncing</u>-> to pronounce

(2) <u>had a lunch</u> -> had lunch

(3) <u>have your car go</u> -> have your car going

(4) <u>repairing</u> -> repaired

166. (1) <u>on mathematics</u>-> with mathematics

(2) <u>to marry with</u> him -> to marry him

(3) <u>continuing</u> -> to continue

(4) <u>to pursue</u> -> from pursuing

167. (1) <u>John comes</u> -> comes John

(2) <u>There again you go</u> -> There you go again

(3) <u>Here my bus comes</u> -> Here comes my bus

(4) <u>from a country to a country</u> -> from country to country

168. (1) <u>to sing and dance</u>-> singing and dacing

(2) <u>to write</u> -> writing

(3) <u>to tavel</u> -> traveling

(4) <u>to climb</u> -> climbing

169. (1) <u>How does he look like?</u>-> What does he look like?

(2) <u>How was...</u> ->What was ....

(3) <u>critical for</u> -> critical of

(4) <u>I am to be blamed</u> -> I am to blame

# Answers for Section C. Find an error in each sentence.

170. (1) opened-> open

(2) close -> closed

(3) to have -> to having

(4) than to go out -> than go (going) out


171. (1) time-honorable -> time-honored

(2) is called as a museum -> is called a museum

(3) Taking a great pride of -> Taking great pride in

(4) on the display -> on display


172. (1) pride of -> pride in

(2) take care for -> take care of

(3) to cut down drinking -> to cut down on drinking

(4) near to the museum ->  near the museum


173. (1) performing -> to perform

(2) him with $300,000 -> him $300,000

(3) in building -> to build

(4) secceeded to -> secceeded in the exam


174. (1) him to help me -> to him for help

(2) for one's field -> in one's field

(3) asking -> to ask

(4) Secured -> Securing


175. (1) He is wiser than handsome. -> He is more wise than handsome.

(2) ran on Mary ->ran into Mary

(3) driving by -> driven by

(4) on the wheel -> at the wheel


176. (1) whom -> with whom or together with

(2) responsible of- > responsible for

(3) for the shopper -> to the shoppers

(4) are my friend -> is my friend

# Answers for Section C. Find an error in each sentence.

177. (1) so young -> too young

(2) know -> knows

(3) in facing -> to face

(4) come to age -> come of age

178. (1) developing -> to develop

(2) the thought to go back -> the thought of going back

(3) for this region -> of this region

(4) the matter for -> the matter with

179. (1) lacking at -> lacking in

(2)  discussed about our... -> discussed our holiday schedules

(3) in snow -> in the snow

(4) on several reasons -> for several reasons

180. (1) married with -> married to

(2) How long ago were you -> How long ago have you been married?

(3) was married -> got married

(4) engaged with -> engaged to

181. (1) over the imminent dangers -> of the imminent dangers

(2) to keep by -> to keep or to abide by

(3) the most historical -> the most historically

(4) warned the people for -> warned the people of

182. (1) go a travel -> go on a travel

(2) went for a trip -> went on a trip

(3) a travel over -> a travel around the world

(4) If giving a chance -> Given a chance

183. (1) keep eyes -> keep an eye

(2) is cheating -> was cheating

(3) I took my picture -> I had my picture taken

(4) Seeing from -> Seen from

# Answers for Section C. Find an error in each sentence.

184. (1) <u>I ever met</u> -> I have ever met

(2) <u>taught him with how to...</u> -> taught him how to treat ....

(3) <u>across with a variety of</u> -> across a variety of

(4) <u>but tender-hearted</u> -> but is tender-hearted

185. (1) <u>mind to open</u> -> mind opening

(2) <u>cry alone</u> -> crying alone

(3) <u>Focus</u> -> Focus on

(4) <u>well off to stay</u> -> well off staying in the dormitory

186. (1) <u>finished to work</u> -> finished working

(2) <u>to not wake</u> -> not to wake

(3) <u>Despite of</u> -> In spite of / Despite

(4) <u>not same</u> -> not the same

187. (1) <u>in needs</u> -> in need

(2) <u>in the trouble</u> -> in trouble

(3) <u>to do</u> -> doing

(4) <u>woman to cry</u> -> woman cry

188. (1) <u>they are</u> -> it is

(2) <u>on colorful flowers</u> -> with colorful flowers

(3) <u>is very famous</u> -> is so famous

(4) <u>by the eye-popping view</u> -> at the eye-popping view

189. (1) <u>getting married</u> -> to get married

(2) <u>enough deep</u> -> deep enough

(3) <u>with using a broomstick</u> -> using a broomstick or with a broomstick

(4) <u>in shape with my brother</u> -> in shape to my brother

190. (1) <u>since I had left the town</u> -> since I left the town

(2) <u>by ten minutes</u> -> in ten minutes

(3) <u>with time</u> -> with the time

(4) <u>is visiting</u> -> is (to) visit

# Answers for Section C. Find an error in each sentence.

191. (1) most -> the most

(2) for you -> with you

(3) lacks of common sense -> lacks in common sense

(4) out gas -> out of gas

192. (1) she goes to -> she went to

(2) than was expected -> than expected

(3) I never expected -> I've never expected

(4) very -> so

193. (1) went -> goes (runs)

(2) died with -> died of

(3) a breaking leg -> a broken leg

(4) let go from -> let go of

194. (1) in charge to -> in charge of

(2) responsible to -> responsible for

(3) lays -> lies

(4) cannot afford neglecting -> cannot afford to neglect

195. (1) troubled from -> troubled with

(2) came to the rescue -> came to rescue

(3) sat in -> sat up

(4) were disappeared -> disappeared

196. (1) made friend with ->made friends with

(2) changed bus -> changed buses

(3) Your scissor is -> Your scissors are

(4) the shoes store -> the shoe store

197. (1) your production -> your productivity

(2) wise for you -> wise of you

(3) foolish you -> foolish of you

(4) you took a break -> you (should) take a break

# Answers for Section C. Find an error in each sentence.

198. (1) <u>help understood</u> -> help understand

(2) <u>work hardly</u> -> to work hard

(3) <u>like women</u> -> so wemen

(4) <u>Frankly spoken</u> -> Frankly speaking


199. (1) <u>his job</u> -> their jobs

(2) <u>you want to work</u> -> you want to work in (at)

(3) <u>appeal you</u> -> appeal to you

(4) <u>that you are coming</u> -> if you are coming


200. (1) <u>how to deal with</u> -> how to play

(2) <u>to play hide and seek</u> -> playing hide and seek

(3) <u>are</u> -> were

(4) <u>sitting down</u> -> to sit down


201. (1) <u>in the winning team</u> -> on the winning team

(2) <u>before reaching</u> -> from reaching

(3) <u>and voted</u> -> and was voted

(4) <u>by two and three</u> -> by twos and threes


202. (1) <u>in my mind</u> -> in mind

(2) <u>every clever</u> -> so clever

(3) <u>for you</u> -> on you

(4) <u>with the pink dress</u> -> in the pink dress


203. (1) <u>celebrated</u> -> are celebrated

(2) <u>marks on</u> -> falls on

(3) <u>Today checks</u> -> Today marks

(4) <u>red-lettered days</u> -> red-letter days


204. (1) <u>in heavy Korean accents</u> -> with heavy Korean accents

(2) <u>in English</u> -> of English

(3) <u>in which</u> -> with which

(4) <u>mother's tongue</u> -> mother tongue

# Answers for Section C. Find an error in each sentence.

205. (1) <u>the book the best</u> -> the book as the best

(2) <u>the flower of</u> -> as the flower of

(3) <u>very strong</u> -> so strong

(4) <u>My uncle was used to life me up...</u> -> My uncle used to lift me up...

206. (1) <u>about</u> -> of / on

(2) <u>having</u> -> to have

(3) <u>My sister was majored in</u> -> My siser majored in

(4) <u>lost an interest</u> -> lost interest

207. (1) <u>was interested him</u> -> interested him

(2) <u>on graduate school</u> -> in graduate school

(3) <u>for</u> -> in

(4) <u>on the field</u> -> in the field

208. (1) <u>by success</u> -> with success

(2) <u>for the English test</u> -> on his English test

(3) <u>referred to</u> -> refer to

(4) <u>until late night</u> -> until late at night (last night)

209. (1) <u>I appreciate you for the help</u>-> I appreciate your help/ I thank you for your help

(2) <u>think him being a good friend</u>-> thank him to be a good friend/ think of him as a....

(3) <u>I am grateful you for your kindness</u>-> I am grateful to you for your kindness

(4) <u>due with</u> -> due to

210. (1) <u>I hope your wish come true</u> -> I hope your wish comes true / will come true

(2) <u>I wish I am rich!</u> -> I wish I were rich!

(3) <u>came on</u> -> came about

(4) <u>in the mind</u> -> in mind

# Answers for Section C. Find an error in each sentence.

211. (1) <u>for trifling things</u> -> on trifling things

(2) <u>wise for you</u>-> wise of you

(3) <u>by they get a job</u> -> until they get a job

(4) <u>to cope for</u> -> to cope with


212. (1) <u>on</u> -> off

(2) <u>to watch others</u> -> to watching others

(3) <u>in endowed on</u> -> is endowed with

(4) <u>spoken highly</u> -> spoken highly of


213. (1) <u>Thanking to</u> -> Thanks to

(2) <u>remained to be intact</u> -> remained intact

(3) <u>tells</u> -> says

(4) <u>was denied with access</u> -> was denied access


214. (1) <u>will be never able to</u> -> will never be able to

(2) <u>at June</u> -> in June

(3) <u>by Kimchi</u> -> without Kimchi

(4) <u>cleared up</u> -> cleaned up


215. (1) <u>since</u> -> from

(2) <u>at his making...</u> -> for his making...

(3) <u>at shool</u> -> from school

(4) <u>on bike</u> -> by bike


216. (1) <u>when I had</u> -> before I had

(2) <u>in the Korean history</u> -> on the Korean history

(3) <u>at TV</u> -> on TV

(4) <u>lately</u> -> late


217. (1) <u>waited</u> -> waiting

(2) <u>live up at</u> -> live up to

(3) <u>children to stay up</u> -> children staying up

(4) <u>do business</u> -> doing business

# Answers for Section C. Find an error in each sentence.

218. (1) <u>in a brush</u> -> with a brush

(2) <u>in the pencil</u> -> in pencil

(3) <u>in the red</u> -> in red

(4) <u>in airplane</u> -> by airplane

219. (1) <u>incapable to walk up</u> -> incapable of walking up

(2) <u>person</u> -> person to person

(3) <u>with huge amount of money</u> -> with a huge amount of

(4) <u>not much successful</u> -> not so much successful

220. (1) <u>broke out with</u> -> break up with

(2) <u>not to go</u> -> not go

(3) <u>beside his capability</u> -> above his capability

(4) <u>figure up</u> -> figure out

221. (1) <u>Yes I believe</u> -> Yes, I do

(2) <u>get rid</u> -> get rid of

(3) <u>would be led to</u> -> would lead to

(4) <u>stick on</u> -> stick to

222. (1) <u>I will donate</u> -> I would donate

(2) <u>finished up</u> -> ended up

(3) <u>pay for</u> -> pay off

(4) <u>Ten million dollars are good...</u> -> Ten million dollars is good....

223. (1) <u>at mowing</u> -> on mowing

(2) <u>from then</u> -> since then

(3) <u>terribly</u> -> terrible

(4) <u>was living</u> -> was alive

# Answers for Section C. Find an error in each sentence.

224. (1) <u>by this time</u> -> at this time

(2) <u>during several days</u> -> for several days

(3) <u>a trip of Hawaii</u> -> a trip to Hawaii

(4) <u>in</u> -> on

225. (1) <u>left to</u> ->  left for

(2) <u>is bound to</u> -> be bound for

(3) <u>being a good losesr</u> -> to be a good loser

(4) <u>is good for</u> -> is good at

226. (1) <u>made friend</u> -> made friends

(2) <u>curious on</u> -> curious about

(3) <u>take care for</u> -> take care of

(4) <u>than better </u> -> than good

227. (1) <u>no concern in</u>-> no concern for

(2) <u>have been studied </u> -> have studied

(3) <u>to go</u> -> going

(4) <u>for the piano</u> -> at the piano

228. (1) <u>the taller</u> -> the tallest

(2) <u>the harder</u> -> hardest

(3) <u>the brightest than any other in the class</u> -> the brightest in the class / brighter than any other one in the class

(4) <u>whoever that wins the race</u> -> whoever wins the race

229. (1) <u>mind to lend</u> -> mind lending

(2) <u>is not above</u> -> is not beyond

(3) <u>are to be blamed</u> -> are to blame

(4) <u>is called as</u> -> is called

230. (1) <u>with casting votes</u> -> by casting votes

(2) <u>deprived with</u> -> deprived of

(3) <u>voted with</u> -> voted for

(4) <u>for the genral election</u> -> in the general election

# Answers for Section C. Find an error in each sentence.

231. (1) <u>discuss about our holiday</u> -> discuss our holiday / have a discussion about our holiday

(2) <u>is lackng of</u> -> is lacking in

(3) <u>to go on a swim</u> -> to go for a swim (cf. to go swimming)

(4) <u>awaited for</u> -> awaited / wait for

232. (1) <u>the form with ink</u> -> the form in ink

(2) <u>the form with balck ink</u> -> the form in black ink

(3) <u>difficulty in</u> ->difficulty with

(4) <u>being looked in</u> -> being looked at

233. (1) <u>ended down</u> -> ended up

(2) <u>traded with</u> -> traded in

(3) <u>a visit at</u> -> a visit to

(4) <u>I wish we didn't give in</u> -> I wish we hadn't given in

234. (1) <u>to mine</u> -> to me

(2) <u>to be absent from</u> -> for being absent from

(3) <u>on the world</u> -> around the world

(4) <u>going out</u> -> going out with

# Answers for Section C. Find an error in each sentence.

235. (1) <u>What time he was coming did he say?</u> -> What time did he say he was coming?

(2) <u>Why are you so happy about?</u> -> What are you so happy about?

(3) <u>It is a boring place to live!</u> -> It is a boring place to live in

(4) <u>Do you think who is the brightest boy?</u> -> who do you think is the brightest boy?

236. (1) <u>took the responsibility</u> -> take the responsibility

(2) <u>stayed behind</u> -> stay behind

(3) <u>his men fellowed</u> -> his men follow

(4) <u>followed his driections</u> -> follow his directions

237. (1) <u>raising</u> -> raised

(2) <u>How was</u> -> What was

(3) <u>aware of</u> -> aware that

(4) <u>found herself was in love</u> -> found herself in love...

238. (1) <u>Keep eyes on</u> -> Keep an eye on

(2) <u>I asked that she...</u> -> I asked if she was.....

(3) <u>something to write</u> -> something to write with

(4) <u>by accidents</u> -> by accident

239. (1) <u>basing on its quality</u> -> based on it quality

(2) <u>clloecting</u> -> to collect

(3) <u>play violin</u> -> play the violin

(4) <u>beside your job</u> -> besides your job

240. (1) <u>ten days are required</u> -> ten days is required

(2) <u>the tireder we get</u> -> the more tired we get

(3) <u>comparing to</u> -> compared to

(4) <u>"Never I will to it, mom."</u> -> "Never will I do it, mom."

# ABOUT THE EDITOR

LIKE TEST PREP

# Free Bonus 1

## Preview of '240 Writing Topics with Sample Essays'

240 WRITING TOPICS

WITH SAMPLE ESSAYS

LIKE TEST PREP

## Q121. Which season—winter, spring, summer, or fall—is your favorite? Why?

## A. Essay Outline

Argument: Summer is my favorite season.
Support 1: I have a lot of free time in the summer.
Support 2: There's more daylight so I can play longer.
Support 3: The summer is always very warm.
Thesis: Because it's easier to have fun in the summer, I like summer the best.

## B. Model Essay

I would have to say that summer is my favorite season of all. First off, it means that school is out and I can do whatever I want. Next, it means that there are more daylight hours to enjoy. And thirdly, summer is a time to enjoy being outside in the warm sunshine. Summer is my favorite season of all because of these reasons.

First of all, summer is when school is out and I can spend all of my time playing both outside and in. My parents encourage me to get out in the sunlight as much as possible and this is fine since my friends and I like to go out together and have a good time. We like to go out and go exploring on our bikes, usually through the woods outside our neighborhood. Of course, it rains quite frequently in the summer as well, so we usually try to hang out in one another's houses. We always have a great time together in the summer, because we have all the time we need to have fun.

Another thing that makes summer my favorite season of all is that there's more daylight hours to enjoy. The sun stays out longer, usually sometime after eight in the evening. This means that there's a lot more sunshine to be out in and enjoy while going out and having fun. I can go swimming in the sunlight or just lay and get a suntan, so long as I don't do it for too long, I don't want to get burned. The sun is the reason why we go out and it just means we can be out longer during the summer.

The last reason is that it's the warmest time of year for us and we don't get very much warm weather where we come from. For most of the year, it's usually cool and wet or cold and icy. We only have three months of reprieve from the chill and wet and that is summer. When my neighbors and I want to celebrate the summer, we go out, have barbecues, or just sit and talk outside. This is a good thing to do at night, when the heat of the day lingers in the night air. So the warmth of the summer air is a rare treat for us and we relish it when it comes around each year.

So summer is my favorite season of all because it's the time of year that really puts together everything I like to do and experience. There's no school in the summer so we can really have all the fun we want during the day. There's more daylight during the day so there's more day to enjoy. And the warmth of summer is something we only have a limited time to enjoy throughout the rest of the wetter, colder parts of the year for us. That's why summer is my favorite season.

## C. Useful Expressions

1. I would have to say that summer is my favorite season of all.

_____

2. My parents encourage me to get out in the sunlight as much as possible, and this is fine since me and my friends like to go out together and have a good time

_____

3. Of course, it rains quite frequently in the summer as well, so we usually try to hang out in one another's houses.

_____

4. I can go swimming in the sunlight or just lay out and get a suntan, so long as I don't do it for too long.

_____

5. We only have three months of reprieve from the chill and wet and that is summer.

_____

6. This is a good thing to do at night, when the heat of the day lingers into the night air.

_____

_____

7. So the warmth of the summer air is a rare treat for us and we relish it when it comes around each year.

_____

_____

8. So the summer is my favorite season of all because it's the time of year that really puts together everything I like to do and experience.

_____

_____

9. There's no school in the summer so we can really have all the fun we want during the day.

_____

_____

10. And the warmth of summer is something we only have a limited time to enjoy throughout the rest of the wetter, colder parts of the year for us.

_____

_____

_____

# Free Bonus 2

# Visit www.liketestprep.com and www.sunshinebooks.co.kr And sign up for our email services on new books and free e-books!!!

# Free Bonus 3

Visit <u>www.liketestprep.com</u>
and
<u>www.sunshinebooks.co.kr</u>
And get free Audio mp3 files
and more downloads!!!

# LIKE TEST PREP Series

## Advanced Reading, Writing, and Grammar for Test Prep

1. Teaches you how to do better on reading and writing tests
2. Tips based on reading, writing, and grammar research
3. Vocabulary, Sample Questions, and Question Type Analysis

## 480 Model Essays

480 Challenging Essay Questions and Sample Essays

## 480 Model Critiques

480 Model Critiques on 480 Model Essays

## 480 Writing Topics with Sample Essays

480 Essay Questions and Sample Essays

## 480 Speaking Topics with Sample Answers

480 Speaking Questions and Sample Answers

## 480 Writing Summaries

480 Reading/Listening Summary Questions & Sample Summaries

## 480 Speaking Summaries

480 Speaking Questions and Sample Summaries

## 240 Basic Writing Topics

480 Basic Essay Questions and Sample Essays

## 240 Basic Speaking Topics

480 Basic Speaking Questions and Sample Answers

## Meet Amazing Americans Workbook Series

Meet Amazing Americans Workbook for http://www.americaslibrary.gov/aa/

# LIKE/Sunshine Publishing

## 200 Korean Dialogues

Master Basic and Intermediate level daily conversations

## Korean for Children 1-3

Children can learn Basic and Intermediate level Korean.

## Open Door to English Book 1-6

Pre, K-6, or ESL/EFL K-6 students can enjoy learning Basic level English through musical dialogues. Videos (DVDs and downloads) and Audios are available.

## English for Kids Book 1-4

Pre, K ESL/EFL students can enjoy learning Basic level English through fun songs.

Videos (DVDs and downloads) and Audios are available.

## English for Children 1-3

Pre, K-6 ESL and EFL Children can learn Basic level English.

## Aesop's Fables 1-4

K-6, ESL and EFL students can learn Intermediate level English through Aesop's Fables and songs.

## 200 English Dialogues

Master Basic and Intermediate level daily conversations in English.

Great for ESL (English as Second Language) Learners

## Proverbs for Preschoolers

Young Children can learn good moral values through proverbs for Pre, K-6

## All True Stories: 33 Life Lessons

Heart touching short stories told by In-hwan Kim, Ph.D.

Made in the USA
San Bernardino, CA
17 November 2015